ALDEN CLAMOR

Osho's Wisdom on Aloneness: The Art of Being Alone According to Osho

Embrace Aloneness and find love, creativity, and authenticity within

First published by Alden Clamor ~ 8, Women's Club St, Barangay San Isidro, 1113-NCR, Quezon City, Philippines ~ Contact number: +639560332409 ~ Published: 2024

First edition

This book was professionally typeset on Reedsy.
Find out more at reedsy.com

Contents

Introduction

Have you ever felt utterly alone in a room full of people? This paradoxical experience, so familiar yet unsettling, raises profound questions about our connection with ourselves and the world. Years ago, I found myself adrift in the bustling streets of Europe, surrounded by the unfamiliar and the unknown. Despite the animated crowds, a penetrating sense of solitude enveloped me. At first, this solitude felt like an uninvited guest that I neither wanted nor understood. During these moments of profound isolation, I stumbled upon Osho's teachings.

Aloneness, often misconstrued as a dreary physical condition, carries the seed of self-realization within it. **There is a profound difference between being alone and feeling lonely.** Osho, a visionary thinker, invites us to reconsider aloneness not as a state of lack but as a rich opportunity for self-discovery and enlightenment. **As I ventured deeper into his insights, a transformation unfolded within me.** What was once a source of discomfort became a sanctuary of peace and self-acceptance. **As I continued to read and reflect, his words were like seeds that began to sprout and revealed to me the transformative power of aloneness.** In the quiet moments of aloneness, we can hear the whispers of our true selves, unfiltered by the cacophony of societal expectations. **Aloneness is not a state of deficiency; it is a state of completeness.**

This book seeks to unravel Osho's rich tapestry of insights on the art of being alone—a journey from the outer noise to the inner silence. In this book, I aim to guide you through the nuances of being alone as Osho saw it. We will explore how aloneness can serve as a canvas for **self-compassion or self-love,** a space where **creativity** flows freely, and a foundation for **authenticity or authentic connection with oneself** and, ultimately, the world.

Again:

In this book, I aim to guide you through the nuances of being alone as Osho saw it. We will explore how aloneness can serve as a canvas for self-compassion or self-love, a space where creativity flows freely, and a foundation for authenticity or authentic connection with oneself and, ultimately, the world.

This journey is designed for you, whether you are a Baby Boomer, a Gen Xer, a Millennial, or a Gen Z. Each generation faces its unique challenges but shares a common yearning for meaning and connection. **You are not alone in this journey**.

Structured to walk you through various dimensions of aloneness, each chapter of this book builds upon the last, crafting a comprehensive map to help you navigate your personal landscape of self-discovery. From learning to sit with discomfort to uncovering the joy in moments of solitude, we will delve into practical steps that foster a deeper understanding of oneself and cultivate a fulfilling relationship with aloneness. You will not just read about aloneness but also be equipped with tools to thrive in it.

This book is for all who have ever felt alone. It offers a fresh perspective that promises comfort and a profound, transformative experience. Therefore, let us step together into being alone, not as a condition to be feared but as a remarkable state to be lived fully and consciously.

Let us go on this journey with an eager spirit, ready to transform aloneness from a state of lack to abundant self-awareness and interconnectedness. As we embark on this exploration, we will discover that aloneness is not a void to be feared but a space brimming with potential. It is an opportunity to face our deepest fears and align with our highest aspirations. It is an opportunity to embrace the full spectrum of our humanity. Through the wisdom of Osho, we will learn to see aloneness as a gift instead of a curse, a gateway to self-discovery and authentic living instead of a dreary dead end. Welcome to a journey that could change how you view aloneness and how you live each moment of your life. **In embracing aloneness, you will find peace, love, creativity, completeness, and your authentic self.**

Chapter 1: Why Being Alone Is Important

" Loneliness is the absence of the other. Aloneness is the presence of oneself... Aloneness is presence, overflowing presence." - Osho Osho's words echo through the chambers of the heart that yearn for understanding. In the solitude of our own company, we encounter the raw materials for love, creativity, and greatness. In the crucible of aloneness, we forge our true identity, away from the din and cacophony of the external world. This emphasis on aloneness as a tool for self-discovery invites us to be reflective and self-aware.

Osho said that the capacity to be alone is the capacity to love. He said that only those who are alone can be creative because creativity needs space and silence. **He also said that greatness is attained by those who dare to be alone and that the deeper secrets of life open their doors only in solitude.**

Osho observed that many live as mere shadows of their potential, confined by the chains of conformity. **They conform because they are insecure. They are insecure because they live in fear.** They breathe, yet they do not live. They exist, yet they do not thrive. They are not really alive because they are not themselves. They are living according to the expectations, opinions, and judgment of others. **However, as Osho believed, aloneness is the key to breaking free from these chains.** It is the path to liberation, empowering us to live authentically and without fear.

Osho advocated for embracing aloneness to break free from these chains. In the depths of solitude, we can unearth the essence of our being and the path to our unique destiny. **Osho understood that being alone is not a state of lack but a state of abundance.**

Again:

Osho understood that being alone is not a state of lack but a state of abundance.

It means being abundantly aware of yourself, being in touch with your essence, and being aware of your potential. **If we want to live fully, we need to be alone. We need to be alone because only then can we discover who we are, what we want, and what we can do.** This transformative power of aloneness is possible when we align with the Source within. Because within us lies a power bigger than us.

Again:

If we want to live fully, we need to be alone. We need to be alone because only then can we discover who we are, what we want, and what we can do. This transformative power of aloneness is possible when we align with the Source within. Because within us lies a power bigger than us.

The importance of being alone lies in the fertile ground it provides for self-reflection and inner dialogue. It is the canvas upon which we can paint our thoughts and dreams without the rough brushstrokes of judgment. Aloneness is the soil in which the seeds of creativity sprout, nurtured by the waters of introspection and the sunlight of clarity.

Aloneness is not merely important but essential for anyone seeking to live a life of purpose and passion. Aloneness is the foundation for authentic relationships, as only those comfortable in their skin can genuinely connect with others.

Aloneness plays a crucial role in fostering a creative spirit, as the quietude of solitude is where inspiration speaks with the most force.

By understanding the significance of aloneness, we begin to shed the societal stigma attached to it and start to appreciate the richness it brings to our lives. We learn to cherish the moments of solitude as opportunities for growth and transformation, leading us to a deeper connection with ourselves and the world around us. Being alone means being independent, self-reliant, and self-responsible. Being alone means being authentic, original, and unique. And only then can we connect with existence deeply, intimately, and joyfully.

I will often mention Baby Boomers, Millennials, Gen Xs, and Gen Zs in this book. To help you get a lay of the land, here's a summary of the different generational classifications and their corresponding birth years:

- Silent Generation: Born between 1928-1945
- Baby Boomers: Born between 1946-1964
- Generation X (Gen X): Born between 1965-1980
- Millennials (Gen Y): Born between 1981-1996
- Generation Z (Gen Z): Born between 1997-2012
- Generation Alpha: Birth years are still debated but commonly cited as starting from the early 2010s up to 2025

These classifications are based on research by organizations like the Pew Research Center and are widely accepted for demographic studies. Each generation is shaped by their time's cultural, social, and economic events, influencing their collective attitudes and behaviors.

Chapter 2: The Fear of Aloneness

The fear of aloneness is as ancient as humanity itself. It whispers tales of abandonment and casts shadows of doubt into our hearts. It is a fear that Osho understood deeply and addressed with compassion and insight. **Osho suggests that one should not be afraid of being alone but rather enjoy it as a gift.** He said that being alone can help one meditate, discover oneself, and be free from the conditioning of others. He said being alone can make one more authentic, more compassionate, and more loving.

2.1 Understanding the Fear

Why do we fear being alone? At its core, the fear of aloneness is rooted in our primal need for connection and survival. In the early days of human history, being alone could mean vulnerability to the elements and predators. **In the early days, being alone could mean death.** Today, while the physical dangers may have diminished, the psychological impact remains potent. **We fear being judged, being seen as outcasts, or facing the mirror of our thoughts and feelings without the distractions of company.**

2.2 Society's Amplification of the Fear

Modern society often amplifies this fear, equating solitude with social failure. The constant barrage of social media and the glorification of busyness make aloneness seem like an anomaly. Mainstream media is constantly selling the idea that happiness is found in the external—the perfect relationship, the bustling career, the vibrant social life. **That being complete is to seek someone outside us. That we are not complete without another. That without the other, I am nothing.** This is a LIE. This external focus can lead to a neglect of our inner world (which is the real source of our power), making the prospect of facing it alone daunting.

2.3 Osho's Perspective on Overcoming the Fear

Osho invites us to view aloneness not as a source of fear but as a source of strength. He encourages us to embrace solitude as an opportunity for self-discovery and transformation. **To overcome the fear of aloneness, Osho suggests a radical shift in perspective—from seeing aloneness as a lack to seeing it as a presence, abundance, and fullness of being.**

When you embrace aloneness as a source of strength, you will find time to be alone whenever you find an opportunity to do so.

2.4 To help us on this journey, Osho highly recommends that we meditate:

Start by spending some time every day in silence and solitude. Find a quiet place where you can sit comfortably and relax. Close your eyes and breathe deeply. Let go of all thoughts and feelings. Just be aware of your breathing and your body sensations.

Gradually increase the duration and frequency of your silent moments. Try to spend at least 30 minutes every day in silence and solitude. And occasionally, you can also spend a whole day or Saturday and Sunday in silence and solitude.

Use your silent moments as opportunities to meditate.

Meditation is not a technique or a ritual. **It is simply a state of awareness, witnessing, and watching yourself without judgment or interference.** Meditation is the way to know yourself.

When you meditate, don't try to achieve anything or change anything. Don't try to stop your thoughts or control your emotions. **Don't attempt to achieve any goals or pursue any moments of joy.** Just watch whatever happens inside you with curiosity and compassion.

As you meditate regularly, you will notice that your mind becomes calmer and clearer. You will notice that your emotions become more balanced and harmonious. You will notice that your body becomes more relaxed and healthy.

As you meditate regularly, you will also notice that your sense of self changes. You will realize you are not your thoughts, feelings, or body sensations. You will discover that you are something deeper, something beyond words or forms or names.

As you meditate regularly, you will notice that your sense of existence changes. You will realize that you are not separate from others, from nature, or the whole. You will discover that you are part of a larger reality, a cosmic consciousness, a divine presence.

2.5 Embracing Aloneness as a Gift

As we apply these practices, the fear of aloneness begins to dissolve, revealing the gift that it truly is. **We start to appreciate the silence that once unnerved us and find joy in the company of our soul.** Aloneness becomes a cherished companion on the path to self-realization.

Chapter 3: The Benefits of Being Alone

loneness, as Osho teaches, is a fertile ground for personal development and self-discovery. There are myriad benefits from embracing aloneness and learning to enjoy one's own company. He said being alone can make us more creative, loving, and free. He said that being alone can help us to find our purpose, to fulfill our potential, and to enjoy our existence.

Here are some of the benefits that being alone can bring. In the succeeding chapters, I will mention practical tips on how to embrace aloneness in your daily life:

3.1 Creativity Unleashed

In the silence of aloneness, the mind can wander and explore without boundaries. The mind is unshackled, free to roam the vast landscapes of imagination without borders. **This freedom is the fertile soil from which the seeds of creativity sprout.** This boundless freedom is the birthplace of creativity. **Osho taught that true creativity is born from a wellspring of inner stillness—a sanctuary where the incessant chatter of the external world is silenced, and the whispers of our deepest thoughts and ideas can be heard.**

Aloneness is the canvas upon which our innermost visions can be painted, a stage where the drama of our untold stories can unfold. It is a realm where expression is unfiltered, raw, and authentic, unmarred by the fear of judgment or the chains of inhibition. Here, in the solitude of our own presence, we are free to explore the uncharted territories of our psyche, to play with the abstract, to discover new ideas, insights, and solutions, **and to give form to the formless**.

It is in this quietude that our minds become fertile grounds for innovation. **Aloneness does not stifle; it breathes life into our creative impulses.** It is the crucible where new ideas are forged, where insights crystallize into clarity, and where solutions emerge from the depths of contemplation. **Each revelation, each spark of ingenuity, is a testament to the power of aloneness to fuel the fires of creativity.**

Let us embrace the silence of aloneness, for it is in this space that the symphony of creativity is composed. Each note resonates with the possibility of discovery, each melody sings of the potential that lies within. In the stillness, we find the freedom to create, to innovate, and to transform the whispers of our soul into the masterpieces of our existence.

3.2 Self-Love and Acceptance

Aloneness provides the space to get to know oneself intimately. In the tranquil embrace of aloneness, we are afforded a precious opportunity to meet ourselves in the most intimate settings, allowing us to learn to accept and love ourselves fully. **This solitude is not loneliness but a sanctuary where the soul can commune with the self.** Here, in the gentle quiet of our own company, we can embark on the most profound journey of self-discovery and self-acceptance.

Osho emphasized that the cornerstone of all love is rooted in the fertile soil of self-acceptance. It is the foundation for extending love to others. **It enhances our love because it teaches us to love ourselves first.** It is the understanding that before we can extend our love outward, we must first cultivate it within. Aloneness nurtures this self-love, allowing it to blossom and flourish. **It teaches us to embrace our imperfections, to celebrate our uniqueness, and to acknowledge our worth.**

This transformative journey of self-acceptance is a testament to the power of self-love. **Our capacity to love others expands exponentially as we learn to love ourselves.** Again:

Our capacity to love others expands exponentially as we learn to love ourselves.

Our relationships are no longer tethered by the chains of attachment or marred by the shadows of expectation. Instead, **they become expressions of our inner abundance**, reflections of the confidence and self-assurance that self-love has instilled within us.

In the quiet moments of aloneness, we learn that self-love is not selfish but the highest form of generosity. When we love ourselves, we fill our cup to the brim, and from this place of overflow, we can share our essence with the world. This self-love is a beacon, guiding us through the ebbs and flows of life, **reminding us that we are enough, just as we are.** Self-love and acceptance empower us to share ourselves with others without attachment or expectation, instilling a sense of confidence and self-assurance.

Let us cherish the gift of aloneness, for it is the crucible in which the gold of self-love is refined. It is the mirror that reflects our true self, the teacher that shows us the beauty of our soul, and the path that leads us to the heart of who we are. **In embracing aloneness, we find the freedom to be our most authentic selves; in this authenticity, we discover the power to love unconditionally.**

3.3 Freedom from Social Conditioning

In the quietude of aloneness, we find ourselves at a vantage point, free from the relentless march of societal expectations and conditioning. It is a space where the shackles of conformity are loosened, allowing us to step back and critically examine the mosaic of beliefs and values that have been handed down to us. Being alone allows one to step back from the beliefs and thoughts hammered into one's head. It offers a chance to question, and redefine one's beliefs and values, and examine one's thoughts, leading to a more authentic and liberated existence.

Aloneness is a powerful tool that empowers us to question the status quo, to peel back the layers of societal norms that have been draped upon us since birth. It is a chance to hold each belief up to the light of scrutiny and ask,

"Does this resonate with my true self?" This introspective journey leads us to a more authentic and liberated existence, **one that is crafted with intention rather than inherited by default.** It liberates us from the often mesmerizing influence of society, culture, religion, or family. It allows us to choose our path, values, and way of living.

Consider the societal scripts about career choices, gender roles, or personal relationships—these narratives can be powerful, yet they often come from a place outside of our desires. For instance, the expectation of pursuing a high-paying job even though you hate the job and would love to do something else, conform to traditional family roles, or follow a certain relationship model. Aloneness empowers us to challenge these scripts, to write our own stories that reflect our individuality and aspirations.

Again:

Consider the societal scripts about career choices, gender roles, or personal relationships—these narratives can be powerful, yet they often come from a place outside of our desires.

In the sanctuary of aloneness, we can liberate ourselves from the pervasive influence of society, culture, religion, or family. **Here, we are not actors playing a part written by others; we are the playwrights, the directors, and the stars of our lives. Aloneness does not isolate us; it frees us.**

Again:

Aloneness does not isolate us; it frees us.

Aloneness grants us the courage to choose our path, to select the values that resonate with our soul, and to embrace a way of living that is in harmony with our most profound truths.

Let us rejoice in the freedom that aloneness brings, for it is a crucible in which we can melt away the dross of external expectations and pour forth the pure gold of our unique individuality. It is the garden where we can cultivate the flowers of self-determination, each petal a choice, each bloom a declaration of our autonomy.

In the embrace of aloneness, we are not adrift in a sea of societal dictates;

we are the captains of our ship, navigating the waters of life with a compass calibrated to our north star. Here, in the silence of our solitude, we discover the boundless freedom to be **unapologetically** ourselves. Let us not forget the profound benefits of aloneness: the freedom to choose our own path, the power to define our values, and the joy of living in harmony with our deepest truths.

3.4 Discovering Purpose

Aloneness can be a powerful ally in uncovering one's life purpose. **Without the noise of external influences, aloneness can connect us with our essence, where one can better listen to the inner voice, which is often described as a gut feeling or intuition, that guides us toward our true calling.** Aloneness is a powerful ally, a guiding star leading us to the discovery of our life's true purpose. Stripped of the cacophony of external influences, aloneness offers us the clarity and tranquility to connect with the very core of our being, bringing a sense of calm and peace.

Here, in the quietude of aloneness, the inner voice—that subtle whisper of intuition—becomes a resonant call. Often manifested as a gut feeling, this voice is the compass of the soul, pointing unwaveringly towards our north star. It is in this space of introspection that we can attune ourselves to its guidance, allowing it to illuminate the path to our true calling and reveal our true nature, unique gifts, and deepest passions. **Aloneness empowers us to follow our heart and intuition, instilling a sense of confidence and self-assurance.**

This voice, a blend of wisdom and desire, reveals the tapestry of our true nature, the unique gifts we possess, and the most profound passions that set our hearts ablaze. It is the beacon that cuts through the fog of uncertainty, revealing the landmarks of our destiny.

Aloneness does not leave us adrift; it anchors us to the essence of who we are. It encourages us to follow our heart and trust the intuition that knows our capabilities and potential even when in doubt. It is the mentor that teaches us to be courageous in the pursuit of what sets our soul on fire.

By embracing the solitude that aloneness provides, we embark on the

most important journey of all—the journey inward. Here, we discover the seeds of purpose planted within us, waiting to be nurtured by our attention and intention. Aloneness is not a void; it is a garden where the flowers of purpose bloom, offering their fragrance to guide us on our way.

Let us cherish this sacred space of aloneness, for it is the crucible in which our purpose is forged, the silent retreat where our life's mission is whispered to us on the winds of introspection. Here, we are the seekers and the finders, the dreamers and the doers, united in the quest to live a life of meaning and fulfillment.

3.5 Realizing potential

Aloneness challenges individuals to push beyond their comfort zones and realize their full potential. It is in aloneness that one can set goals, reflect on progress, and cultivate the growth, evolution, and discipline needed to achieve greatness. Aloneness invites us to face our fears, overcome our limitations, and transcend our boundaries.

We stand at the crossroads of self-discovery and self-mastery in the hallowed halls of aloneness. Here, in the serenity of our own company, **the seeds of our latent potential begin to sprout.** Aloneness is not just a state of being; it is a crucible for transformation, challenging us to stretch the fabric of our capabilities and weave the tapestry of our destiny.

Within the embrace of aloneness, we are the architects of our aspirations. It is the fertile ground where we plant the goals that reach for the stars, the sanctuary where we reflect on our journey's milestones and the forge where we temper the steel of our resolve. **In this sacred space, growth is not just an option—it is the only direction.**

Again:

In this sacred space, growth is not just an option—it is the only direction.

Aloneness beckons us to confront the specters of our fears, to stare into the abyss of our doubts, and to emerge victorious. It is the chisel that sculpts our character, carving away the excess to reveal the masterpiece within. **We are**

called to overcome the barriers we have built, to leap over the walls that confine us, and to soar into the expanse of our true potential.

This solitary voyage is a pilgrimage towards greatness. **It inspires an insatiable thirst for learning, a relentless pursuit of knowledge and wisdom, and an unwavering commitment to skill mastery.** It inspires us to learn new skills, acquire new knowledge, and master new abilities. Each new ability we acquire is a star in the constellation of our capabilities, guiding us through the night of uncertainty.

In aloneness, we are the alchemists of our existence, transmuting the leaden weight of complacency into the golden light of achievement. **We are summoned to transcend the ordinary, molding the clay of our being into a work of art that is a testament to the human spirit's sovereign will.**

Let us embrace the solitude that shapes heroes, the aloneness that forges legends. For it is in the depths of our inner world that we uncover the boundless realm of possibility, and it is from this wellspring of solitude that we draw the power to realize our full potential.

3.6 Experiencing Joy

Osho taught that joy is an intrinsic part of being. In aloneness, we become more aware and appreciative of things around us. **We can find joy in the simplest of life's offerings, in life's various forms and manifestations.** He says that joy is woven into the very fabric of our existence. It is not a transient visitor, but a constant companion, awaiting our recognition. In the sacred sanctuary of aloneness, we are invited to a banquet of awareness, where every moment is an opportunity to savor the richness of life. **This heightened sense of joy leads to a more content and fulfilled existence, bringing us peace and bliss.**

As we embrace aloneness, our senses awaken to the symphony of existence. The rustling leaves speak in hushed tones of ancient wisdom, the crimson hues of the sunset paint our inner canvas with awe, and the gentle caress of the breeze reminds us of the tender touch of the cosmos. **In these moments, joy is no longer a concept but a palpable presence that dances around us,**

within us.

Aloneness becomes a chalice, overflowing with the nectar of appreciation for the myriad expressions of life. We find joy in the mundane—a dewdrop glistening on a blade of grass becomes a jewel of the morning sun, and a smile from a stranger transforms into a silent sonnet of connectedness. **This heightened sense of joy is not fleeting; it is a steady flame that warms the soul, guiding us toward a state of contentment and fulfillment.**

In this embrace of aloneness, we discover that joy is not dependent on the external but is a reflection of our inner landscape. It is the blossoming of peace that roots itself in the depths of our being, spreading its petals to touch every aspect of our lives. **This joy is the essence of bliss—a serene harmony that resonates with the rhythm of the universe, a testament to the beauty of simply being.**

Through the teachings of Osho, we learn that this joy is our birthright, an ever-present gift that enriches our journey, making each step an act of celebration, each breath a chorus of gratitude. **In the stillness of our solitude, we are not alone; we are united with all of existence, partaking in the eternal dance of joy.**

AN INVITATION TO BE CO-CREATOR WITH ME

f you have reached this far, then I invite you to be my co-creator.

Unlock the Power of Generosity

"Friendship is the purest love. It is the highest form of Love where nothing is asked for, no condition, where one simply enjoys giving." – Osho

People who give without expectation live longer, happier lives and make more money. So if we've got a shot at that during our time together, darn it, I'm gonna try.

To make that happen, I have a question for you...

<u>Would you help someone you've never met, even if you never got credit for it?</u>

Who is this person you ask? They are like you. Or, at least, like you used to be. Less knowledgeable, doubtful, wanting to make a difference, and needing help, but unsure where to look.

My mission is to make this book "Osho's Wisdom on Aloneness" accessible to everyone. Everything I do stems from that mission. And, the only way for me to accomplish that mission is by reaching... well... everyone.

This is where you come in. Most people do, in fact, judge a book by its cover (and its reviews). So here's my ask on behalf of a struggling Baby Boomer, Gen X, Millennial, or Gen Z you've never met:

Would you like to be a **co-creator with me** in spreading the wonderful wisdom of this book "Osho's Wisdom on Aloneness" to the world? Your voice can resonate where mine cannot, **reaching ears I may never whisper to**. Together, we can amplify the message of this book and touch the hearts of countless individuals searching for guidance on their journey to self-discovery.

Please help that Baby Boomer, Gen X, Millennial, Gen Z by doing a Review of this book.

Your gift costs no money and takes less than 60 seconds to make real, but it can change a fellow Baby Boomer, Gen X, Millennial, or Gen Z's life forever. Your doing a Review could help...

...one person feel more confident and empowered.
...one more father inspire his family.
...one more mother inspire her family.
...one more client transform their life.
...one more dream come true.
...one more person discover their true self.

To get that 'feel good' feeling and help this person for real, all you have to do is...and it takes less than 60 seconds... do a Review of this book from the Store or Online Store where you bought this book.

Thank you from the bottom of my heart. Now, back to our regularly scheduled reading.

Your biggest fan, Alden Clamor

PS – Fun fact: If you provide something of value to another person, it makes you more valuable to them. If you'd like goodwill straight from another Baby Boomer, Gen X, Millennial, or Gen Z – and you believe this book will help them – <u>send this book their way</u>.

Chapter 4: Aloneness in Various Cultures

Aloneness is a concept that transcends cultural boundaries, yet each culture has its unique perspective. This chapter explores how different societies view and value aloneness, providing a broader understanding of its role in human experience.

4.1 Eastern Philosophies

In Eastern philosophies, notably Buddhism and Taoism, aloneness is not merely a state of being physically alone but a profound experience that can lead to spiritual awakening and enlightenment. **This concept is deeply rooted in the understanding that true peace and understanding come from within rather than from external sources.**

Buddhism emphasizes the importance of solitude in pursuing Dharma (cosmic law and order), as it allows for deep meditation and reflection free from the distractions of the social world. Meditation in seclusion is a way to cultivate mindfulness, compassion, and wisdom. **It is believed that through solitary practice, one can achieve Nirvana, the ultimate state of liberation from suffering and the cycle of rebirth.**

Conversely, Taoism views aloneness as a means to harmonize with the Tao or the fundamental nature of the universe. The Taoist sage seeks to understand the flow of nature and align with it. Aloneness is valued as a time for introspection and connection with the natural world, fostering a deep sense of unity with all things. In this way, aloneness becomes a path to achieving Wu Wei, or effortless action, acting by the Tao.

Both philosophies believe that aloneness can lead to a profound under-standing of one's place in the cosmos and the interconnectedness of all life. By embracing aloneness, one can strip away the illusions and distractions of the ego, allowing for a clearer perception of reality and a deeper connection with the divine. **This path is not seen as lonely or isolating but rather as a journey towards self-realization and cosmic harmony.**

4.2 Western Individualism

In the Western world, aloneness is often intertwined with the cultural values of individualism and self-reliance. These values are deeply embedded in Western thought and society, shaping how aloneness is perceived and experienced.

An emphasis on the autonomy and self-determination of the individual characterizes individualism in the West. **It is the belief that each person is unique and should have the freedom to pursue their goals and express their identity.** In this context, aloneness is seen as an opportunity for self-discovery and personal growth. It is a time when individuals can focus on their interests, develop their skills, and reflect on their personal beliefs without the influence of others.

Self-reliance is another cornerstone of Western culture, often associated with the ability to be independent and self-sufficient. Ralph Waldo Emerson famously articulated the concept in his essay "Self-Reliance," arguing that individuals should trust themselves and their intuition rather than conform to societal expectations. **In this sense, aloneness is valued as a state where one can cultivate resilience and the capacity to handle life's challenges without relying on external support.**

However, it's important to note that while aloneness can be empowering and fulfilling, in the Western context, it can also be associated with loneliness and social isolation. **The balance between enjoying solitude and maintaining social connections is a nuanced aspect of Western life.** While some may find solace and strength in being alone, others may struggle with loneliness when separated from community and companionship.

The Western perspective on aloneness reflects a complex interplay be-

tween celebrating individual freedom and the human need for social interaction. It underscores the importance of finding a personal equilibrium between solitude and society, where one can enjoy the benefits of aloneness without succumbing to the potential drawbacks of isolation.

4.3 Indigenous Wisdom

Indigenous cultures have often revered aloneness as a sacred time for personal and spiritual growth. This respect for solitude is deeply woven into their traditions and rituals, serving as a bridge to deeper understanding and connection with the universe.

Rites of Passage

Many indigenous societies incorporate periods of solitude into rites of passage. These are crucial times when an individual transitions from one stage of life to another, such as childhood to adulthood. During these times, the individual may spend time alone in nature, often fasting and meditating, to receive guidance from the spirit world. This practice, sometimes called a **vision quest,** is believed to help individuals clarify their purpose and role within their community.

Wisdom from Ancestors

In indigenous cultures, ancestors hold a place of high honor and are considered a source of wisdom and guidance. Solitude allows individuals to communicate with their ancestors through prayer, meditation, and dreams. It is a time to listen to the voices of those who have passed on, to seek their advice, and to honor their memory.

Connection with the Natural World

Indigenous people often view themselves as part of a larger ecosystem, deeply connected to the land and its creatures. Aloneness in the natural world is a way to strengthen this connection, to learn from the environment, and to understand the intricate web of life. **It is believed nature itself communicates and offers insights that can only be heard in the stillness of being alone.**

In these cultures, aloneness is not seen as isolation but as an integral part of the human experience. It is a time for reflection, learning, and profound personal transformation. **Through aloneness, one can tap into the collective wisdom of the community, the ancestors, and the Earth, fostering a sense of belonging and responsibility to the greater whole.**

4.4 Modern Interpretations

In the modern era, the concept of aloneness has taken on new dimensions with the rise of technology and global connectivity. These advancements have reshaped how we experience solitude and integrate the ancient wisdom of aloneness into contemporary life.

Technology and Connectivity: While technology has made it easier than ever to stay connected with others, paradoxically, it has also allowed for a new kind of solitude. Social media and instant communication can create an illusion of companionship without the depth of interaction, leading to feeling alone in a crowded digital space. **However, technology also offers tools for self-reflection and personal growth, such as meditation apps and online resources for self-improvement, aligning with the ancient practices of introspection and self-discovery.**

4.5 Work and Lifestyle

With its increasing acceptance of remote work and flexible schedules, the modern work environment has created more opportunities for individuals to spend time alone. This shift is a return to the ancient value of solitude, providing space for creativity and problem-solving without the distractions of a traditional office setting. Yet, it also challenges individuals to balance and maintain social connections outside work.

4.6 Urbanization and Personal Space

As urbanization grows, the quest for personal space becomes more pronounced. In densely populated cities, finding moments of solitude can be a respite from the hustle and bustle of city life. Parks, libraries, and other public spaces offer urban dwellers a chance to be alone with their thoughts, echoing the ancient practice of seeking solitude in nature.

4.7 Mindfulness and Well-being

There is a growing recognition of the importance of mindfulness and mental well-being in modern society. This has led to a resurgence of interest in practices that promote aloneness as a way to de-stress and reconnect with oneself, such as yoga, meditation retreats, and solo travel. These activities draw on the ancient understanding of aloneness as a time for rejuvenation and spiritual nourishment.

In reconciling the ancient wisdom of aloneness with contemporary lifestyles, modern society finds new ways to value and incorporate solitude. **While the context has changed, the core idea remains: aloneness can be a powerful catalyst for personal transformation and a deeper understanding of one's place in the world.** It is a timeless concept that continues to evolve, offering each generation a path to self-awareness and inner peace.

Chapter 5: Embracing Solitude as Strength

5.1 Aloneness vs. Loneliness: Redefining Terms for a Healthier Perspective

Aloneness is not the hollow echo of emptiness; it is a fullness, a presence that fills the space with the essence of our being. It is a chosen state, a sacred time we give to ourselves, where the only voice we hear is our own, and the only presence we feel is the pulsating life within us - Source within us.

In aloneness, we find strength—not the strength that roars, but the strength that whispers and stands firm in the face of life's storms. This strength does not come from the company of others but from our soul, which is forever connected with Source. In these quiet moments, we gather the scattered pieces of ourselves, weaving them into a tapestry of self-awareness and inner peace.

As we redefine the terms of our existence, aloneness becomes a sanctuary, a retreat from the world's demands. Here, in the stillness, we build our fortress of peace, where we can retreat to find clarity and purpose. The societal stigma that once shadowed our alone time dissipates, and we emerge, embracing our solitude without guilt or explanation. **This redefinition is not just a shift in perception, but a powerful act of self-empowerment.**

Our solitary journey is not a path we walk in isolation but one we navigate with the understanding of those who share our lives. We learn to balance the expectations of family and society with our need for solitude, **communicating**

our boundaries with love and clarity. This open communication is key to harmonizing our inner world with the outer, creating a symphony of solitude that enriches every aspect of our being.

We find inspiration and courage through the stories of those who have walked this path before us. **We see that aloneness is not a barrier to success but a bridge to creativity and fulfillment**. These narratives guide us, showing us how to use our alone time to **thrive, create, and grow**. They remind us that aloneness is not a burden, but a gift that can inspire and empower us.

We learn that aloneness is not something to be endured but to be celebrated, a gift we give to ourselves, a time when we can indeed be free. This celebration of aloneness is a testament to our strength and a declaration of our independence.

5.2 The Strength in Stillness: How to Harness Solitude for Personal Growth

As we continue to weave the narrative of aloneness' strength, we arrive at the heart of stillness—a place where the quiet is not empty but rich with possibility. Here, in the embrace of aloneness, we find a reservoir of resilience that empowers us to grow beyond the confines of our everyday lives.

In this stillness, we are not stagnant; we are in motion, moving inward to the core of our being. It is a journey of introspection, where each silent moment is a step towards self-awareness and personal evolution. **Aloneness becomes our teacher, instructing us in the art of contemplation and the discipline of thought. It is a space where we can confront our fears, challenge our limitations, and celebrate our victories—all in the company of our most authentic selves.**

The strength found in aloneness is not loud or boisterous; it is a quiet power that comes from within. It is the strength to face the world on our terms, make decisions that resonate with our most genuine intentions, and live a life aligned with our deepest values. This strength is cultivated when we step away from the noise and into the serenity of our presence.

Yet, embracing this strength requires courage—the courage to stand

apart from the crowd, to resist the pull of constant connectivity, and to find contentment in our own company. It is a courage that grows with each solitary moment, with each breath of freedom that fills our lungs in the quiet corners of our existence. This courage is not just a virtue but a necessary tool in our journey of self-discovery.

As we journey through the chapters of aloneness, we learn to harness this strength for our personal growth. **We discover that the stillness of being alone is not a void to be filled but a canvas to be painted with the colors of our imagination and the brushstrokes of our desires**. Aloneness, then, is not just a state of being; it is a state of becoming—becoming more robust, wiser, and more attuned to the whispers of our hearts.

5.3 Overcoming Social Stigma: Embracing Alone Time Without Guilt

In the unfolding narrative of aloneness' embrace, we encounter the challenge of societal perceptions. **Aloneness is often misjudged as a sign of social deficiency rather than a deliberate choice for personal enrichment.**

The journey into aloneness is a personal odyssey that may be misunderstood by those who view aloneness through a lens of concern. Yet, it is in the quiet defiance of these misconceptions that we find true freedom. **Aloneness is not a retreat from society but an advance into the self, a bold step into the space where we are free to explore, reflect, and be**.

To navigate the waters of social expectations, we must anchor ourselves in the truth of our experience. Aloneness is not a plight to be pitied but a choice to be celebrated. It is a testament to our strength, a declaration of our independence, and a celebration of our autonomy. In the sanctuary of aloneness, we are not lost but found, not empty but full, not lacking but complete.

As we embrace our alone time, we learn to shed the weight of guilt that society has draped upon us. We understand that aloneness is a gift, a precious time that allows us to recharge, renew, and return to the world with a clearer vision and a lighter heart. It is a time when we can honor our needs, set our boundaries, and cultivate a relationship with ourselves that is both nurturing and empowering.

Through the art of aloneness, we challenge the stigma, rewrite the narrative, and emerge with a newfound appreciation for life's quiet moments. These moments are not interruptions in our social existence but integral parts of a balanced life—where aloneness and social engagement dance harmoniously, each enriching the other.

5.4 Solitary Activities that Boost Creativity and Self-Reflection

In the solitude of our own company, we discover a wellspring of creativity and a mirror for self-reflection. This section of our journey illuminates the solitary activities that nourish the mind and invigorate the soul, allowing us to flourish in the quiet.

Aloneness is the artist's studio, the writer's den, the thinker's garden. It is where the seeds of creativity are sown and nurtured, away from the prying eyes and bustling sounds of the outside world. In this sacred space, the mind can wander to explore the vast landscapes of imagination without restraint or censure. Here, the brush strokes are bolder, the words more profound, and the thoughts clearer.

The act of creation in aloneness is a dialogue with the self, a conversation that can be both challenging and rewarding. It is a process of discovery, where each solitary activity becomes a stepping stone towards a greater understanding of our capabilities and potential. Whether through the meditative practice of painting, the rhythmic strumming of a guitar, or the reflective solitude of a nature walk, each experience enriches us, providing a more profound sense of connection to the essence of who we are.

Yet, the path to harnessing creativity in aloneness has its challenges. It requires the courage to face the blank page, the empty canvas, the silent instrument, and see not an intimidating void but a realm of possibilities. It demands the resilience to push through moments of doubt and the persistence to continue creating even when inspiration seems elusive.

As we embrace the solitary activities that boost our creativity and self-

reflection, we learn to appreciate the silence not as an absence of noise but as the presence of an opportunity to create, reflect, and grow. Aloneness becomes a cherished companion on our creative journey, a trusted confidant in our quest for self-expression and personal evolution.

5.5 Managing Family Expectations on Being Social

As we continue to narrate the story of aloneness' embrace, we arrive at a point where the individual must navigate the delicate balance between personal solitude and family expectations. This part of the journey is about finding peace in aloneness and harmonizing this need with the social fabric of family life.

Aloneness, while a personal sanctuary, often requires negotiation within the family context. Here, we must articulate the value of our alone time, not as a rejection of family but as an essential component of our well-being. Balancing aloneness with family expectations is akin to a dance that requires grace, understanding, and clear communication.

In this dance, we learn to set boundaries with compassion, ensuring that our need for aloneness is respected while honoring the relationships that enrich our lives. We strive to educate our loved ones about the benefits of aloneness, sharing how it replenishes our spirit and enhances our capacity to connect more meaningfully with others.

Yet, the path has its challenges. We may encounter resistance or misunderstanding, guilt for desiring time apart, or the struggle to maintain harmony when our needs seem at odds with family dynamics. But it is through these very challenges that we grow, learning to assert our needs while remaining empathetic to the needs of those we hold dear.

As we weave the narrative of aloneness and family, we discover that the strength gained in aloneness does not isolate us but empowers us to engage more fully with our loved ones. It is a strength that allows us to be present, to listen deeply, and to share ourselves with authenticity and love.

Chapter 6: Aloneness and Mental Health

This chapter delves into the profound benefits of aloneness as a therapy, a sanctuary where one can find solace and clarity, and a powerful balm for the mind.

6.1 Aloneness as a Therapy: Practical Steps to Mental Wellness

In the quietude of our own presence, we discover that aloneness has the transformative power to soothe the weary mind and mend the frayed edges of our mental tapestry. It is in these moments of undisturbed solitude that we can gently unravel the knots of our thoughts and emotions, laying them out in the light of self-compassion and understanding. Here, in silence, we are both the healer and the healed, the seeker of the sanctuary and the sanctuary.

Aloneness as therapy is a practice, a deliberate act of self-care that allows us to step back from the cacophony of life and listen to the subtle rhythms of our inner world. It is a time to breathe deeply, rest, and rejuvenate. In the embrace of aloneness, we find the space to heal, grow, and emerge renewed, ready to face the world with a renewed purpose and vitality.

Yet, this therapeutic journey requires intention and mindfulness. It calls for us to carve out moments of aloneness with the same dedication we give to our most cherished commitments. **We learn to schedule aloneness, to create rituals around it, and to honor it as a sacred appointment with ourselves. In doing so, we affirm that our mental wellness is a priority, deserving of time and space.**

Again:

We learn to schedule aloneness, to create rituals around it, and to honor it as a sacred appointment with ourselves. In doing so, we affirm that our mental wellness is a priority, deserving of time and space.

As we navigate the delicate balance between aloneness and engagement, we become attuned to the signs that guide us—signs that tell us when aloneness is healing and when it may tip into loneliness. **We become skilled in reading the language of our psyche, understanding when to seek the company of others and when to retreat into the comforting arms of solitude.**

Through the practice of aloneness as therapy, we embark on a path of self-discovery and healing, a journey that leads us to a deeper understanding of our minds and hearts. **It is a journey that teaches us the value of stillness, the wisdom of introspection, and the transformative power of solitude.**

6.2 Mindfulness Practices to Enjoy Alone: Building a Routine

Our exploration of aloneness and its impact on mental health continues, with a focus on the crucial role of mindfulness. Mindfulness practices are not just exercises in concentration, **but acts of reverence for the present moment, enriching our experience of life in the quiet spaces of our solitude.**

Mindfulness in aloneness becomes a symphony of awareness, each note a breath, each pause a heartbeat. It is the practice of anchoring ourselves in the 'now.' **Observing the world within and around us with a gentle curiosity that asks for nothing but our presence.** In the stillness of being alone, we learn to listen—to the rustle of leaves, the rhythm of our breathing, the dance of thoughts across the canvas of our minds.

Building a routine of mindfulness in aloneness is akin to cultivating a garden of tranquility in our inner landscape. We start with the seeds of intention, watering them with regular practice, and nurturing them with patience. As our routine takes root, we find that the fruits of mindfulness—clarity, calm, and compassion—begin to flourish, enriching our experience of aloneness and enhancing our profound connection to the world.

Yet, this practice has its challenges. Like the sea, the mind can be tumultuous, with waves of distraction and currents of restlessness. But with each mindful breath, we learn to navigate these waters, to find peace amidst the storm. We become adept at returning to the breath, finding stillness amidst motion, and cultivating a sense of inner peace that endures beyond our moments of aloneness.

As we delve deeper into mindfulness, we find that it is not an escape from reality but a deeper engagement with it. It is a tool that sharpens our perception, heightens our senses, and opens our hearts. In embracing mindfulness, we find that aloneness is not a void but a vessel filled with the essence of life, waiting to be experienced with every mindful step we take.

6.3 Signs Your Alone Time is Healing vs. When It's Harmful

This section beckons us to discern the subtle line between aloneness as a healing sanctuary and when it may become a shadowed path. This discernment is crucial, for aloneness holds the power to both mend and fray the edges of our mental universe. It's vital to recognize the signs of harmful aloneness to ensure we don't lose ourselves in its depths.

The healing signs of aloneness are like a gentle sunrise, bringing warmth and illumination to our inner world. **When aloneness leaves us feeling rejuvenated, with thoughts clearer and emotions more balanced, we know it has served its restorative purpose.** In these moments, we find our true selves, not in the reflection of others' eyes but in the clarity of our own gaze.

Yet, there is a flip side to this coin—a point where aloneness can spiral into a labyrinth of isolation. **When the echo of our thoughts turns into a cacophony of doubts, when the weight of loneliness replaces the peace of being alone, we must heed these signs.** They are the silent sentinels warning us that aloneness, while a healer, can also harm us if we lose ourselves in its depths.

The art of aloneness is not just about seeking refuge in its embrace but also about maintaining a vigilant watch over our well-being. It is about recognizing when the solace of aloneness begins to slip into the solitude of sorrow. **It is about understanding that while aloneness can be a canvas for self-reflection,**

it should not become a prison for the soul.

As we navigate the waters of aloneness, we learn to steer our course with mindfulness, adjusting our sails when the winds of emotions shift. We learn to balance our time alone with the time spent in the company of others to ensure that our solitude remains a source of strength, not a shadow.

6.4 The Role of Meditation in Cultivating Inner Peace

In the tranquil corners of our bustling world lies a hidden treasure, a jewel that Osho often spoke of with great reverence. **It is the treasure of meditation, a simple yet profound practice that can transform the chaos of our minds into a symphony of inner peace.** Meditation has long been revered as a profound practice for achieving inner peace, a state of tranquility that Osho describes as the door to non-violence, love, and compassion. In the serene silence of meditation, one can find a respite from the cacophony of daily life, a sanctuary where the mind can rest and the soul can flourish.

Osho emphasizes that meditation is not about adopting a technique; it's a state of no-mind, a journey beyond thoughts into silence. Here, in the depths of stillness, one encounters the essence of being.

As Osho puts it:

"Silence is not the silence of a cemetery; it is a song without words, a dance without movements." – Osho

Meditation, therefore, is not an escape but a return to the core of our existence, where peace is not just felt but becomes the very fabric of our being.

Imagine a place within you, untouched by the noise and haste of modern life, where every breath ushers in a wave of calm, and every exhale releases the burdens of the soul. This is the sanctuary meditation offers—a return to the essence of being, where the mind is no longer a turbulent sea but a serene lake, reflecting the beauty of the sky above.

Osho taught that meditation is not an act of doing but a state of being. It is not about controlling the mind but witnessing it, **not about reaching**

somewhere but realizing you are already there.

Osho said.

"Meditation is a surrender; it is not a demand... It is not forcing existence to your terms, but meeting existence as it is." - Osho

According to Osho:

"The real question is not whether life exists after death. The real question is whether you are alive before death." -Osho

Again:

"The real question is not whether life exists after death. The real question is whether you are alive before death." -Osho

Are you alive right now? Through meditation, we invite readers to experience this aliveness, to touch the eternal now, and to find within themselves a peace that the world cannot disturb.

6.5 Disconnect to Reconnect: Reducing Digital Overload

In a world where our lives are increasingly intertwined with digital devices, the concept of '**disconnecting to reconnect**' has become vital for maintaining mental health and well-being. **With Osho's profound understanding of the human psyche, he encouraged finding moments of disconnection from the external noise to reconnect with our inner selves.**

Digital overload, the state of being overwhelmed by the constant influx of digital information, can lead to symptoms such as fatigue, burnout, and decreased productivity. It is a phenomenon that affects individuals across the globe as we grapple with the demands of staying informed and connected in a rapidly evolving digital landscape.

Imagine yourself amid your routine surrounded by the hum of technology— the pings of messages, the glow of notifications, the endless scroll of social media. It's a digital dance we all partake in, often unconsciously, as we navigate the data streams that vie for our attention.

Now, imagine taking a step back. You power down your devices, the screen

fades to black, and a hush falls over your world. In this newfound silence, you are afforded the luxury of presence. Once racing to keep up with the digital pace, the mind begins to slow, and in the stillness, you find space—**a space for reflection, creativity, and peace.**

A disconnection from the external to forge a deeper connection with the internal is the essence of what Osho encouraged. It is not a rejection of technology but an invitation to balance. By setting aside time to unplug, we are not losing touch with the world; instead, we are rediscovering the touch of our soul.

In reducing digital overload, we are not merely escaping the noise; we are tuning into the subtle whispers of our inner voice - the most precious voice of all. This voice often gets lost in the din and holds the keys to our authenticity and wisdom. In the moments of solitude, away from the digital clamor, we can hear it most clearly.

The practice of digital detox is not a one-time event but a habit to be cultivated. It might start with designated hours of disengagement, perhaps during meals or before bedtime, gradually expanding to encompass entire days or weekends. **The goal is not rigid abstinence but mindful moderation, an awareness of when to engage and retreat.**

We find ourselves at a crossroads as we continue our journey through the digital wilderness. One path leads back to the familiar territory of constant connectivity, while the other invites us to explore the uncharted landscapes of our inner world. The uncharted landscapes of our inner world are the paths less traveled, and this is the path Osho beckoned us towards—a path of mindful disengagement that promises a reunion with the self.

As we navigate this path, our relationship with technology transforms. We begin to use it with intention, not compulsion. Our interactions become more meaningful, our focus sharper, and our lives richer. **We learn that by turning off, we are turning on**—a deeper awareness, a heightened sense of being, and a more authentic connection to the world around us.

Again:

We learn that by turning off, we are turning on.

We embrace the paradox of disconnection as a pathway to reconnection. It is a journey that leads us back to ourselves, to the core of our being, **where peace is not just a concept but a lived experience.** As we emerge from our digital retreats, we bring a renewed spirit, ready to engage with the world more consciously and thoroughly.

In this tranquility, away from the digital din, we discover the subtle rhythms of our existence. The heartbeat, the breath, the ebb and flow of our thoughts— all become vivid in the silence. **In embracing aloneness, we encounter the most profound connection of all: the connection to our authentic selves.**

Osho's teachings remind us that every moment of disconnection is an opportunity to reconnect with the life force that animates us. **He urged us to find the spaces between our thoughts, for it is in these spaces that the seeds of peace and creativity are sown.** As we cultivate these seeds through meditation and mindfulness, we watch them blossom into a tranquil garden.

The art of disconnecting is not about severing ties with the world but about redefining our relationship with it. **It is a dance of presence, where we learn to be fully in the moment, whether offline or online.** We reclaim our power over our attention and time by consciously choosing when to engage with the digital realm.

This narrative is not just a story but an invitation to embark on a personal odyssey. It is a call to venture inward, to the place where all journeys begin and end.

In the words of Osho:

"Aloneness is the presence of oneself. Aloneness is very positive. It is a presence, overflowing presence. You are so full of presence that you can fill the whole universe with your presence, and there is no need for anybody." - Osho

So, let us heed the call, turning the pages of our lives with intention and grace. Let us disconnect, not to isolate, but to delve deeper into the essence of who we are. And as we do, we find that our digital devices become empowerment tools rather than distraction, conduits for connection rather than separation.

Ultimately, we emerge from our digital sabbaticals refreshed and renewed, carrying with us the wisdom of aloneness. We return to the world with a new perspective, ready to engage with technology not as enslavers or enslaved people but as conscious participants in the dance of life. In this dance, we find harmony, balance, and peace that flow from the inside out, touching every aspect of our existence.

6.6 Personal Stories: Transformation Through Solitude

In the tapestry of life, each thread tells a story, and in the realm of solitude, these stories often speak of profound transformation. Osho, a master of inner alchemy, illuminated the path to self-discovery by embracing aloneness. He taught that aloneness is not a state of emptiness but a rich landscape brimming with the potential for personal growth.

Let us weave together the narratives of those who have walked this path, individuals from all walks of life who found a wellspring of creativity, love, and authenticity in their aloneness. These are the stories of transformation that occur when we step back from the world and look within.

The Hermit's Solitude

In a verdant expanse where the forest whispers secrets of the ancient earth, there stood a modest hut, a sanctuary for a solitary hermit. This sage, draped in the simplicity of his existence, had renounced the cacophony of societal life for the serenity of nature's embrace. His days were not marked by the sun's journey across the sky but by the depth of his meditation and the breadth of his contemplation.

The Villagers' Curiosity

The villagers from the nearby hamlet often pondered over the hermit's reclusive lifestyle. Their lives, woven with the threads of communal bonds and daily toils, contrasted starkly with his. They speculated amongst themselves, crafting tales of his past and prophecies of his enlightenment. Yet, none dared to breach the silent perimeter of his abode, save for the whispers of the wind carrying their distant voices.

The Young Man's Inquiry

One crisp morning, as dew still clung to the leaves and the dawn chorus filled the air, a young man entered the hermit's domain. Driven by an insatiable curiosity that outshone the trepidation of his peers, he approached the hermit with a question that had burned in the hearts of many: "Do you not feel lonely in this quiet forest?"

The Hermit's Wisdom

The hermit, opening his eyes that mirrored the stillness of the pond nearby, regarded the young man with a gentle gaze. **"Loneliness," he began, "is a companion of those who seek solace in others without first seeking it within themselves.** In the silence of these woods, where the symphony of life unfolds in its purest form, I have discovered the richest company – **the company of my soul.** It is here, amidst the untouched beauty of creation, that I converse with the essence of life and find kinship with the universe."

The Lesson Learned

The young man left the hermit's presence with a heart full of contemplation. As he retraced his steps through the awakening forest, he realized that aloneness could be a wellspring of insight and that within the serenity of one's being lay the answers to the most profound questions of companionship and existence.

The Artist's Retreat

City's Clamor

A renowned artist lived in the heart of a bustling metropolis, where the animation of urban life reverberated through crowded streets. People whispered her name in galleries and admired her in studios, yet a quiet dissonance grew within her. The city's relentless pace, once a fountain of inspiration, had become a mire of distraction. The artist was adrift in a sea of creative stagnation, yearning for fresh air to rekindle the embers of her passion.

The Journey to Solitude

Determined to escape the oppressive grip of concrete jungles, she embarked on a journey to a place untainted by human artifice. Her destination was a remote cabin nestled in the embrace of the wild. As the city's skyline faded into the horizon, a sense of liberation began to bloom within her. The cabin, a quaint abode of timber and stone, stood as a solitary fortress amidst the vastness of nature's canvas.

Nature's Embrace

Here, the artist found solace in the symphony of the natural world. The whispering leaves, the babbling brook, and the chorus of wildlife became her companions. The solitude she once feared transformed into a profound muse, stirring the depths of her soul. Each sunrise painted the sky with a palette of eager anticipation, and every sunset-inspired reflection of introspection and peace.

The Resurgence of Creativity

The artist's dormant creativity awoke with a newfound vigor in this secluded retreat. Her hands danced with brushes on canvases, capturing the essence of the wilderness that enveloped her. The colors flowed from her core, vibrant and alive, each stroke a testament to her reawakened spirit. Her artworks were not mere images but echoes of her intimate dialogue with aloneness.

The Legacy of the Retreat

The pieces born from this period of seclusion soon traveled beyond the confines of her forest studio, touching the hearts of those who beheld them. They spoke of tranquility and the raw beauty of isolation, earning acclaim as some of her most celebrated works. The artist's retreat into nature's sanctuary became a pivotal chapter in her life, a testament to the power of solitude in unlocking the purest form of artistic expression.

The Traveler's Journey

The Odyssey Begins

In the realm of wanderlust and discovery, there was a traveler whose heart was as vast as the oceans he crossed. His journey was not just a passage through the lands but a voyage into the depths of his spirit. With each step, he traversed beyond the physical distances, venturing into territories uncharted by his predecessors.

Encounters with Diversity

As he meandered through bustling marketplaces, over silent mountains, and across endless deserts, he found himself face-to-face with the myriad tapestries of human existence. Each culture he encountered was a new verse in the poem of humanity, challenging the rigid stanzas of his long-held beliefs. The customs and traditions of the people he met were like keys, unlocking the doors to worlds he never knew existed.

The Transformation

The aloneness of his travels was not a void but a vessel filled with the essence of his experiences. It allowed him to immerse himself in each new day's lessons. The solitude became his teacher and the road, his classroom. With every new language he deciphered and every folklore he heard, his perspective broadened, and his prejudices dissolved.

The Return

When the traveler finally returned from his odyssey, he was no longer the person who had set out on the journey. The aloneness had sculpted him into a being of wisdom and compassion, a mosaic of the cultures and lives he had encountered. He brought back souvenirs, stories, and insights that could inspire change and foster understanding.

The Legacy of the Journey

The traveler's tale became a beacon for those yearning to break free from the confines of their limitations. His journey taught that true wisdom comes from the courage to accept the unknown and that compassion is born from embracing the world with an open heart.

Through this narrative, we are reminded that the journey of self-discovery is the most profound of all travels, and the lessons learned in solitude can illuminate the path to becoming a wise and compassionate individual. ✧

The Scientist's Discovery

The Quest for Knowledge

In the hallowed halls of science, where curiosity intersects with the unknown, there was a scientist whose dedication to discovery was as unwavering as the laws of physics. His laboratory, a labyrinth of beakers and equations, was a fortress against the outside world's distractions. Day and night, he toiled, driven by a relentless pursuit of truth that transcended the need for companionship.

The Laboratory's Solace

The scientist's solitude was not born of isolation but of intention. In the stillness of his lab, among the silent witnesses of test tubes and microscopes, his mind found the clarity it craved. The quiet moments of focused solitude became the crucible for his thoughts, each experiment a step closer to the precipice of innovation.

The Breakthrough

Then, in the waning hours of a starlit night, the pieces of his scientific puzzle aligned. The data merged into a pattern, revealing a profound truth that promised to alter the course of human history. It was a discovery that could only have emerged from the depths of undisturbed contemplation—a testament to the power of a mind left to wander the infinite possibilities of the universe.

The Impact on Humanity

When the scientist unveiled his findings, the world gazed in awe at the simplicity and elegance of his discovery. It was a solution to a problem that had plagued generations, a beacon of hope that illuminated new paths for progress. His work, a product of his aloneness, rippled through the annals of science, touching lives and shaping futures.

The Legacy of Discovery

The scientist's journey was a reminder that solitude can be a fertile ground for the seeds of genius to flourish. The most significant breakthroughs can emerge in the quiet moments of focused solitude, away from the noise of consensus. His story is a testament to the idea that within the silent chambers of the mind, the whispers of discovery echo the loudest.

Through this narrative, we are inspired to appreciate the profound insights that can arise when one dedicates oneself to pursuing knowledge, undeterred by the solitude that often accompanies great endeavors.

The Parable of the Seed

The Seed's Descent

In the realm of parables, where each grain of truth is sown with wisdom, there is the tale of a solitary seed. Unlike its kin, nestled in the nurturing bosom of the fertile earth, this seed tumbled into the abyss of a crevice. In the shadowy confines, it lay alone, enveloped by the cool embrace of the soil and the profound silence of the unknown.

The Darkness as a Cradle

The darkness surrounding the seed was not a harbinger of doom but a cradle for potential. In the absence of light, the seed was not blinded but was instead bestowed with a vision of its destiny. The solitude it faced was not a void but a vast and clean canvas awaiting the strokes of life to render its vibrant masterpiece.

The Emergence of Life

As days passed, the seed's aloneness catalyzed its transformation. It germinated secretly, sending tender roots into the earth's depths and a fragile shoot upwards, questing for the sun. The crack that once seemed a prison became a passage, a narrow gateway leading to the world above.

The Blossoming

Finally, the shoot broke through the surface, and the seed found itself bathed in golden sunlight. It unfurled its leaves, embracing the warmth and the breeze, and in time, blossomed into a flower of such beauty that it captured the gaze of every passerby. Its petals were a testament to the resilience of life, and its fragrance was a whisper of the miracles that solitude can yield.

The Lesson of the Seed

The parable of the seed teaches us that growth often comes from facing the darkness alone. It reminds us that even in solitude, especially in solitude, there is the potential for extraordinary beauty. The seed's journey from the depths of the earth to the world's admiration is a metaphor for the inner strength and splendor that can arise when one is left to flourish in peace.

Through this narrative, we are encouraged to see the value in moments of solitude and recognize that sometimes, **being alone can be the condition needed for the most profound growth and realization.**

The Successful Woman Executive

One such tale is of a woman, a successful executive, who found herself at the pinnacle of her career yet felt an inexplicable emptiness. In the silent moments of a solitary retreat, she discovered her true passion for painting, a talent she had long neglected in pursuing corporate success. Her story is a testament to the creative awakening that solitude can inspire.

The Young Urban Professional

Another narrative unfolds with a young man burdened by societal expectations and the relentless pursuit of material success. In his solitude, he found the courage to shed the masks he wore and embarked on a journey of self-acceptance. Through meditation and reflection, he emerged with a newfound sense of purpose, no longer defined by society's accolades but by his being's authenticity.

Osho's teachings remind us that transformation is not a passive occurrence but an active process of self-reinvention. It is about changing our lifestyle, our patterns of thought, and our interactions with the world. Aloneness offers the space for this transformation, a sacred time to practice, be, and become.

These personal stories and parables are mirrors reflecting the potential within each of us. They serve as a testament to the beauty and strength found in aloneness. They remind us that solitude can be challenging and lead to profound growth and self-discovery. They invite us to ask ourselves: What might we discover if we embrace the aloneness that Osho so eloquently spoke of? How might our lives transform if we allow ourselves the freedom to be alone, to listen to the silence, and to honor the voice that emerges? By embracing aloneness, we open ourselves to a world of possibilities and the potential to create our unique story.

Chapter 7: Philosophical Insights into Aloneness

7.1 Osho on Aloneness: Key Philosophical Teachings Explained

Osho has imparted profound wisdom on the concept of aloneness. His teachings elucidate that aloneness is not a state of deprivation but a moment of richness overflowing with potential. According to Osho, aloneness is the presence of oneself, where one is complete and content in one's being. **In this space of solitude, the individual is not lonely but immensely full, experiencing the totality of existence without needing external validation.**

Osho's perspective invites us to explore the depths of our being and discover the essence of our existence that is untouched by societal influence. He encourages us to embrace aloneness as a path to inner freedom, where one can encounter the true self beyond the roles and identities imposed by the outer world. **In this sacred space, we find that being alone is not a void but a whole universe within, waiting to be joyfully explored.**

Through his teachings, Osho challenges us to redefine our understanding of aloneness and see it as an opportunity for profound spiritual awakening. **He asserts that by embracing aloneness, we can find the keys to unlock our infinite potential and experience the boundless joy that comes from within.** Here, in the quietude of our solitude, we can truly understand the meaning of freedom—**freedom from the chains of social expectations, freedom to**

be our authentic selves, and freedom to live in harmony with the natural rhythm of life.

In the serene landscape of Osho's philosophy, aloneness emerges not as a barren desert of isolation but as a lush oasis of self-discovery and peace. With his penetrating insight, Osho distinguishes between the desolate terrain of loneliness and the verdant groves of aloneness. **Loneliness, he articulates, is a state of lack, a hunger for others' presence, a dependency that echoes the hollows of incompleteness. On the contrary, aloneness is the realization of one's fullness, a silent communion with the self, where one is not alone but deeply connected with the cosmos.** In this sacred solitude, the world's noise fades, and the symphony of the soul begins to play.

Osho beckons us to embrace this aloneness, to find comfort in its stillness, and to recognize it as the fertile ground for meditation and the blossoming of consciousness. He encourages a dive into the depths of being, where one discovers the pearls of wisdom that lie beyond the mind's incessant chatter. **In this profound solitude, Osho assures, lies the key to freedom — freedom from societal expectations, freedom from the mind's limitations, and ultimately, the freedom to be.** It is a journey of shedding the unnecessary, standing naked in the truth of one's existence, and finding joy in the very act of being.

Through the lens of Osho's teachings, aloneness is redefined as a spiritual adventure, a quest that leads to the treasure of existential understanding. **It is not a path of escape but a path of return — a return to the essence, to the heart of existence where one is at once nothing and everything.** In this narrative of aloneness, we are invited to rewrite our stories, not with the ink of societal norms but with the ink of our profound aloneness, crafting a masterpiece of our lives that resonates with authenticity and love.

As we traverse further into the realm of aloneness, Osho's teachings illuminate the path, revealing that this journey is not one of solitude but of profound connection. **In the embrace of aloneness, we encounter the essence of our being — a space where the individual merges with the universal, where the drop becomes the ocean.** Here, in the silence of our inner world, we discover the whispers of truth that have been drowned out by the din and cacophony of life's stage.

Osho guides us to see that the dance of existence is waiting to be realized in aloneness. It is a dance where each step expresses freedom, each movement a stroke of authenticity. **This dance is not choreographed by societal norms but by the rhythm of our hearts**. It is in aloneness that we are invited to dance freely, to explore the movements of our soul without inhibition or fear.

The narrative of aloneness, as painted by Osho, is not a tale of isolation but a celebration of individuality and a testament to the strength within. It is a narrative that encourages us to shed the layers of pretense and to stand in the light of our truth. Aloneness becomes not just a concept but a living experience, a dynamic state of being where every moment is an opportunity for growth and every breath a chance for deeper understanding.

In this sacred space of aloneness, we are not adrift but anchored in the very core of life. Osho's wisdom beckons us to dive into the depths of our aloneness and find the seeds of creativity, the roots of love, and the wings of freedom. Here, in the sanctuary of our solitude, we can flourish, unfurling our potential's petals and basking in the light of self-realization.

7.2 Freedom in Aloneness: What It Really Means

In exploring aloneness, we encounter the concept of freedom—a freedom that is often elusive in the company of others but becomes palpable when we are alone. Osho's teachings illuminate this freedom as an intrinsic part of our being, a state not granted by external entities but discovered within the sanctity of our aloneness.

Osho posits that true freedom arises when we are alone, not in isolation but in the sense of being free from external influences and societal expectations. This aloneness is not a mere physical state but a more profound, existential condition where one finds the courage to live authentically.

Freedom in aloneness is the liberation from the constant chatter of the world, the unshackling of the soul from the expectations and judgments that bind us. It is the space where we can breathe deeply, move freely, and exist authentically. In this sacred space, we are not confined by our roles or the masks we wear; we are ourselves in our purest form.

This freedom is not a destination but a journey that begins with a single step away from the crowd and into the quietude of our presence. It is a path lined with the discovery of our thoughts, untouched by the influence of societal norms. Here, we learn to listen to the rhythm of our hearts and to dance to the beat of our drums.

Osho's vision of freedom in aloneness is not a call to isolation but an invitation to introspection. It is an opportunity to engage with the deepest parts of ourselves, question, challenge, and grow. It is a chance to stand in the light of our truth, unafraid and unapologetic.

Osho's vision of freedom in aloneness is not about detachment from the world but a profound engagement with one's being. In the space of aloneness, we can genuinely listen to our inner voice and follow our path. **This freedom is not an end but a beginning—a gateway to exploring the vastness of our consciousness and the mysteries of life.**

According to Osho, aloneness is the fertile soil in which the seeds of freedom can sprout and flourish. In the quiet moments of solitude, we can break free from the conditioned belief systems and prejudices that limit our capacity to enjoy life in all its richness. **Aloneness provides the clarity and space needed to question, rebel, and ultimately find freedom not defined by others but by our most profound truths.**

7.3 The Zen of Solitude: Lessons on Being Alone but Not Lonely

In the stillness of aloneness, Osho reveals a Zen-like state where one is alone but not lonely. This distinction is crucial in understanding the art of aloneness. Loneliness is a shadow, a reflection of absence, a heartache for the other that is not there. It is a state of lack, a yearning for a company, a dependency on external validation. **As Osho teaches, aloneness is the light that casts that shadow away. It is the presence of oneself, a celebration of one's own company, a contentment that needs no other to complete.**

Osho's teachings guide us through the Zen of solitude, where being alone is an opportunity to meet oneself most intimately. It is a chance to relish one's being, to celebrate life in its purest form—unadorned and unaccompanied. In this space, one is not a fragment longing for wholeness but a complete universe.

The lessons of being alone but not lonely are profound. They teach us that in the silence of our solitude, we can hear the whispers of our deepest desires and the echoes of our most authentic selves. This aloneness is not a void to be filled but a space to be explored—a vast inner landscape brimming with potential and peace.

Through Osho's wisdom, we learn that aloneness is not the absence of noise but the presence of an inner harmony that resonates with the rhythm of existence.

7.4 Aloneness in Eastern vs. Western Philosophies

The contemplation of aloneness has been a subject of profound interest in both Eastern and Western philosophies, each offering its unique lens through which to view this existential state. Eastern philosophy, with its roots deeply embedded in the spiritual soils of India, China, and Japan, often views aloneness as an opportunity for inner reflection and spiritual growth. It is seen as a moment to connect with the universal energies and the self, a time for meditation and the pursuit of enlightenment.

On the other hand, Western philosophy has traditionally approached aloneness from a more analytical standpoint, focusing on the individual's place within the larger social context. The Western perspective often emphasizes the development of the self through interactions with society and the external world, viewing aloneness as a state to be examined and understood through reason and discourse.

Osho offers a unique synthesis in understanding aloneness. He suggests that aloneness is not merely a physical or social condition but a profound psychological and spiritual state that transcends cultural boundaries. According to Osho, whether in the bustling streets of a Western metropolis or the serene ashrams of the East, aloneness is essential for the flowering of consciousness and realizing one's true potential.

Osho's teachings harmonize the Eastern embrace of solitude as a gateway to self-realization with the Western appreciation for individuality and self-actualization. Despite their differing approaches, both philosophies converge on the importance of aloneness as a crucible for personal transformation and cultivating a deeper understanding of one's place in the cosmos.

7.5 Debunking Myths: Osho's Rebuttals to Common Misconceptions

Osho, a master of cutting through societal norms and expectations, often addressed the myths that cloud our understanding of aloneness. He challenged the common misconceptions that aloneness is synonymous with loneliness, signifies social failure, or is a condition to be pitied. Instead, **Osho offered a refreshing perspective that aloneness is a state of great potential and power.**

One of the prevalent myths Osho debunked is the idea that aloneness is a problem that needs to be solved. **He argued that aloneness is not a problem but a solution to the chaos of the mind and the turmoil of the heart.** In aloneness, one finds the clarity and peace that are often elusive in the company of others.

Another misconception Osho addressed is the belief that aloneness leads to disconnection. **On the contrary, Osho taught that aloneness can lead to a deeper connection with oneself and, by extension, with all of existence.** In the space of aloneness, one can truly listen to the rhythm of life and harmonize with it.

Osho also refuted the myth that aloneness is a sign of antisocial behavior or psychological distress. **He explained that aloneness is a natural and healthy state where one can recharge, reflect, and grow.** It is a space where creativity and insight flourish, free from the distractions and judgments of the outside world.

7.6 How Aloneness Improves Your Understanding of Freedom

Osho's teachings often revolve around the intricate relationship between aloneness and freedom. **He suggests that to understand freedom truly, one must first understand aloneness. Aloneness, as Osho describes, is not a mere absence of others; it is a presence, a fullness of being that allows for an authentic experience of freedom.**

In the sanctuary of aloneness, we are free from the expectations and judgments of others. Here, we can shed the layers of social conditioning and discover the essence of our true selves. **Osho emphasizes that this understanding of freedom is not about being unattached or indifferent to the world but about being connected to one's nature so that one can move through the world with grace and ease.**

According to Osho, aloneness is a powerful tool in understanding and experiencing freedom. Aloneness allows us to live with that freedom, to live by ourselves and with ourselves, **and in doing so, we find love and happiness within and with others.** In aloneness, we learn the art of being self-sufficient, not as a means of isolation, but as a means of experiencing the world without dependency.

Osho's perspective on aloneness and freedom challenges us to redefine our understanding of both concepts. **He invites us to see aloneness as an opportunity to embrace our essential condition of freedom, start afresh with ourselves, and redefine our lives' foundations**. In this light, aloneness becomes a transformative force, a revolution of the self that leads to a deeper, more profound sense of freedom.

Chapter 8: Practical Applications of Aloneness

Embracing aloneness is a journey that requires intention and practice. In this chapter, I offer practical steps inspired by Osho's teachings to help you cultivate an enriching and transformative relationship with aloneness. There is actionable advice here to start your practice of embracing aloneness, with an emphasis on creating a personal space and routine that supports solitude.

8.1 Creating a Sanctuary of Solitude

Designate a Space

Identify a space in your home that is your sanctuary for aloneness. It could be a corner of a room, a comfortable chair, a spot on the floor with cushions, or even on your bed. Make it inviting and personal, with a clear sense of purpose in mind.

Set Boundaries

Let your family or housemates know that this space is where you go to be alone. Set clear boundaries about not being disturbed during your aloneness time, empowering yourself and asserting your need for personal space.

8.2 Daily Practices to Cultivate Aloneness and Reap Its Benefits

Osho's teachings emphasize the importance of embracing aloneness as a daily practice, a sacred ritual to connect with one's innermost self. He encourages individuals to dive deep into their aloneness, knowing that it is in this space where true meditation and self-discovery occur. To cultivate aloneness, Osho suggests several practices that can be incorporated into daily life:

Create Moments of Aloneness

Morning Ritual: Begin your day with a moment of solitude. Spend the first few minutes after waking up in silence, setting intentions for the day. This daily practice will bring a sense of accomplishment and set a positive tone for the day.

Evening Reflection: End the day with a period of solitude and reflection. Review the day's events, what you learned, how you felt, the moments of aloneness, and the insights gained. This practice helps to deepen one's understanding of oneself and the benefits of aloneness.

Meditation

Begin each day with a period of meditation. This meditation could be dynamic meditation, a technique Osho developed, which involves stages of breathing, movement, and silence to awaken the life force within. Meditation is the cornerstone of cultivating aloneness, as it allows one to experience the richness of being alone, the silence that speaks, and the flow and focus that come from within. You can start with deep breathing to center yourself. Then listen to yourself breathe. Use guided meditations to help you explore your inner world. There are many resources available online or through apps.

Mindfulness

Throughout the day, practice mindfulness in all activities. Whether eating, walking, or engaging in work, do so with full awareness. **Osho teaches that living in the present moment is the key to experiencing the beauty of the 'now,' where the true essence of life flourishes.**

Mindful Walks

Take solitary walks in nature. Osho believed that being alone in the presence of nature can help one connect with the universal energies and the self. It is a time for reflection and for the soul to commune with the natural world.

Journaling

Keep a journal to document your thoughts, feelings, and insights during moments of aloneness. Writing can be a form of meditation in itself, helping to clarify the mind and allowing for self-expression and self-discovery.

Connecting with Nature

Nature Retreats: Spend time in nature, whether it's a park, the countryside, or your garden. Nature has a calming effect and can enhance the experience of being alone.

Gardening: If you have the space, gardening can be an excellent activity for connecting with yourself.

Creative Expression

Engage in creative activities like painting, writing, or playing music. Osho viewed creativity as a byproduct of a meditative mind, and these solitary pursuits can be a channel for the inner creativity that arises from aloneness. Creativity flourishes in the space of solitude.

Integrating these practices into daily life allows one to cultivate aloneness and experience its profound benefits. Osho's teachings guide us to find joy, creativity, and peace in our solitary moments, transforming them into a source of strength and wisdom.

8.3 Using Alone Time for Deep Meditation Practices

Osho's approach to meditation is unique in its emphasis on using alone time for stillness and dynamic, active engagement with one's inner self. He developed various meditation techniques specifically designed for the modern individual to help break through the layers of the subconscious and connect with the core of one's being.

One such technique is **Dynamic Meditation**, a fast-paced and intense practice involving several stages, each designed to bring about a different state of consciousness. This practice is particularly effective when done alone, as it allows for a more profound and personal experience without external distractions.

The stages of Dynamic Meditation typically include:

Chaotic Breathing: Rapid and deep breathing to build up energy and awaken the dormant life force within.

Emotional Release: Expressing pent-up emotions through movement, sound, or any other form of release.

Hoo Stage: Jumping with arms raised, chanting "Hoo! Hoo! Hoo!" to direct the energy upwards.

Freeze: Stopping all movement suddenly and observing the inner sensations and stillness.

Celebration: Allowing the body to move freely and dance, celebrating the vitality and energy unleashed.

This meditation is best practiced in the early morning, which is traditionally considered a powerful time for spiritual practices due to the quiet and stillness that pervades. The practice can be a profound way to use alone time, transforming it into a period of intense self-exploration and discovery.

Osho also emphasized the importance of **night meditation**. He suggested using the quiet and darkness of the night to sit silently, merge with the surroundings, and meditate on the vastness of the universe. This practice can help one to feel connected to the cosmos and experience a sense of oneness with all that is.

By dedicating alone time to these profound meditation practices, one can embark on a transformative journey that leads to greater self-awareness, emotional release, and a profound sense of inner peace. With their transformative power, Osho's techniques are a potent way to turn inward and discover the boundless joy and freedom that lie within the solitude of one's presence.

8.4 Journaling for Self-Discovery in Aloneness

Osho often emphasized the value of journaling for profound self-discovery. **As a solitary practice, journaling aligns perfectly with his teachings, serving as a mirror to reflect the innermost thoughts and emotions that surface in quiet moments.**

Journaling in solitude offers a private space where one can converse with oneself without reservations. It is an act of self-expression that allows for an honest examination of one's thoughts, feelings, and experiences. Osho believed such practices could lead to a greater understanding of the self and a clearer vision of one's path in life.

In the silence of aloneness, journaling becomes a form of meditation, a way to delve into the layers of the subconscious and bring to light the truths that reside within. It is a practice that encourages mindfulness and presence as one becomes fully engaged in writing, fully absorbed in the present moment.

One can track personal growth, recognize patterns, and clarify intentions through journaling. It is a powerful tool for self-discovery and transformation, as Osho taught that understanding the self is the first step toward change. By documenting the journey of aloneness, you can witness the evolution of your inner being and the blossoming of your spiritual awareness, empowering you with self-awareness and personal growth.

Journaling is a powerful tool for self-discovery, and when practiced in the spirit of Osho's teachings, it can become a profound way to connect with yourself.

8.5 Creative Aloneness: Using Alone Time for Artistic Expression

Osho's teachings on creativity are deeply rooted in the concept of aloneness. He believed true art arises not from the mind but from a state of no-mind, a space of silence and meditation. This creative aloneness is when one can connect with the spontaneous flow of existence, allowing art to emerge naturally without preconception or planning.

In the solitude of one's own space, free from external distractions, the mind can settle, and the inner voice becomes clear. It is in this clarity that creativity flourishes. Osho encouraged individuals to engage in artistic expression as a form of meditation, **where creation is not just about the end product but the process itself**.

Whether one is a painter, a writer, a musician, or a dancer, the key is to let the creativity flow from a place of **inner silence**. This approach transforms the act of creation into meditation, where one is both the creator and the witness to the unfolding of art.

Osho emphasized that creativity should not be confined to traditionally recognized art forms. **Creativity can be found in any activity as long as it is done with joy, love, and a meditative quality.** Cooking, gardening, or even cleaning can become creative acts when performed with this consciousness.

8.6 Physical Wellness Routines You Can Do Alone

Osho's teachings on physical wellness emphasize the interconnectedness of body, mind, and spirit. He advocated for a holistic approach to health, where physical exercises are about maintaining the body and nurturing the soul. According to Osho, physical wellness routines done in solitude can be a form of meditation, a way to connect deeply with oneself and the present moment.

Here are some physical wellness routines inspired by Osho's teachings that can be practiced alone:

Dynamic Stretching: Begin with Dynamic Stretching to awaken the body. Dynamic Stretching involves gentle, flowing movements that stretch and warm up the muscles, preparing the body for more intense activity.

Yoga: Incorporate yoga asanas into your routine. As Osho described, yoga is not just a physical exercise but a science of living. Practice poses that challenge your balance and flexibility, focusing on the breath and the body's alignment.

Breathwork: Engage in deep breathing exercises, or pranayama, to harmonize the body and mind. Osho emphasized the power of breath as a bridge between the conscious and the unconscious, the body and the spirit.

Walking Meditation: Practice walking meditation, where each step is taken with mindfulness and awareness. Osho believed that walking in nature could be a profound meditative experience, bringing one closer to the essence of life.

Dance: **Dance freely, allowing the body to move without inhibition. Osho encouraged da**nce as a celebration of life and a way to express the inner joy that comes from being in tune with oneself.

Self-Massage: End your routine with self-massage, using techniques that promote relaxation and circulation. **Osho taught that loving oneself is the first step towards healing, and self-massage can be a nurturing practice that fosters self-love.**

These routines are designed to be practiced alone, providing a space for introspection and self-care. By engaging in these activities, one can experience the physical benefits of exercise while also enjoying the mental and spiritual upliftment that comes from Osho's holistic approach to wellness.

8.7 The Art of Solo Retreats: Planning Your Personal Escape

Osho taught that taking time for oneself, away from the distractions and demands of daily life, is essential for personal growth and spiritual awakening. **A solo retreat is a perfect opportunity to delve into the practices of meditation, self-reflection, and inner exploration in a focused and uninterrupted manner.**

When planning a solo retreat, consider the following elements inspired by Osho's teachings:

Location: Choose a place that resonates with your need for peace and solitude. It could be a quiet, natural spot, a secluded cabin, or a dedicated meditation retreat center. The key is to find a space that supports introspection and disconnection from the usual routines.

Duration: Decide on the length of your retreat. It could be a weekend, a week, or even longer. The duration should be sufficient to allow you to unwind, go deeper into your practices, and emerge refreshed and renewed, ready to take on life's challenges with a new perspective.

Schedule: Create a loose schedule that includes time for meditation, yoga, reading, and other activities that nurture your spirit. However, remain flexible and open to the spontaneous flow of the retreat experience, allowing yourself the freedom to adapt to your inner needs and desires.

Digital Detox: Commit to a digital detox by limiting or eliminating the use of electronic devices. This practice will help you stay present and reduce distractions, allowing you to engage with your inner journey fully.

Meditation and Mindfulness: Incorporate Osho's meditation techniques into your daily practice. Dynamic meditation, silent sitting, or walking meditation are all powerful tools to deepen your awareness and connect with your inner self.

Journaling: Keep a journal to document insights, emotions, and revelations that arise during your retreat. Writing can be a therapeutic tool for processing and integrating your experiences.

Self-Care: Prioritize self-care by engaging in activities that promote relaxation and well-being, such as self-massage, leisurely walks, or simply resting. These activities are not just indulgences but essential for your overall well-being during the retreat.

Reflection: Allocate time for reflection at the end of each day. Review your experiences, the emotions that surfaced, and the insights gained, using them as a guide for your ongoing personal development.

As Osho envisioned, a solo retreat is a sacred time to reconnect with oneself and the universe. **It's a personal pilgrimage to the core of your being, where you can listen to the whispers of your soul and return with a deeper understanding of your place in the world.**

Planning a solo retreat in the spirit of Osho's teachings can be a transformative experience, offering a chance to reset, recharge, and realign with your true self.

Chapter 9: Challenging Societal Norms

9.1 Why Society Fears Being Alone: A Historical Perspective

Throughout history, aloneness has been a significant aspect of human experience, often viewed with suspicion and fear by society. Osho sheds light on this phenomenon, explaining that being alone forces individuals to confront their true selves. This tradition dates back to the periods of solitude sought by philosophers, mystics, and seekers of truth. He suggests that the fear of aloneness is deeply rooted in our collective psyche, stemming from a time when survival depended on being part of a group.

Osho points out that society acts as a mirror, reflecting a constructed identity that people cling to, avoiding the discomfort of facing their authentic selves. **This fear of aloneness has been perpetuated through cultural narratives and religious teachings emphasizing community and togetherness as virtues, often at the expense of individual self-discovery.**

Historically, moments of solitude have been reserved for philosophers, mystics, and seekers of truth. Figures like Mohammed, Jesus, Mahavira, and Buddha spent periods in solitude to gain profound insights. **Osho argues that such experiences of aloneness are essential for anyone seeking a deeper understanding of life and self-awareness - not only for a Buddha, a Jesus, or a Mohammed.**

Societal structures and cultural norms have shaped our perception of aloneness. **But these structures and norms have misled us. They are keeping us from discovering our true power. It is time to break free and harness our**

own power.

9.2 Osho's Radical Views on Societal Expectations and Aloneness

Osho was known for his radical stance on many societal norms, particularly those related to the expectations placed upon individuals. **He saw societal expectations as a form of bondage that kept people from experiencing their true selves and connecting to the Source within.** According to Osho, society imposes many expectations that create a false sense of identity, leading to suffering when those expectations are unmet.

He argued that the fear of being alone is often a fear of not meeting societal expectations. People are taught to seek validation and meaning through relationships, achievements, and status, which can lead to a perpetual state of dissatisfaction and disconnection from one's inner self. **Osho believed that by shedding these imposed expectations, individuals could discover the beauty and freedom of aloneness.**

Osho's teachings empower individuals to rebel against societal norms, urging them to embrace their uniqueness and to find contentment in their own company. **He saw aloneness not as a state of loneliness but as an opportunity to connect with one's essence beyond the roles and identities shaped by society.** This perspective gives individuals the power to shape their own lives, free from the constraints of societal expectations.

9.3 Navigating Societal Norms While Embracing Aloneness

Osho's teachings often revolved around aloneness as a profound and necessary state for personal growth and enlightenment. He believed that society, with its myriad of norms and expectations, usually opposes the individual's quest for aloneness. According to Osho, society is a construct that distracts individuals from their true selves, creating a fear of being alone that is deeply ingrained in our collective consciousness.

He taught that to truly understand oneself, one must be willing to stand alone and face the world without the crutch of societal approval. Facing the

world without the crutch of societal approval requires courage and a radical shift in perspective. It involves seeing aloneness not as a deficiency but as a space of freedom and self-discovery.

Osho encouraged individuals to question societal norms and to find their path, even if it meant going against the grain. **He saw aloneness as an opportunity to break free from the 'herd mentality',** a term used to describe the tendency of people to conform to a larger group's behaviors and opinions and live authentically to one's inner voice.

This emphasis on independent thinking or critical thinking and action will encourage and empower you to live life on your terms.

9.4 The Transformative Power of Aloneness in Society

Osho's teachings reveal that aloneness can transform the individual and society as a whole. He saw aloneness as a state of being that allows for a profound connection with one's true self, free from societal masks and roles. According to Osho, when individuals embrace aloneness, they become more authentic and, as a result, can contribute to creating a more genuine and compassionate society. **This transformation is not just personal but has the potential to influence the collective consciousness, leading to a more enlightened society.**

He believed that society often fears aloneness because it acts as a mirror, reflecting our true nature in its naked form. This confrontation with the self can be daunting, as it strips away our illusions about who we are. **However, through this process of self-discovery, individuals can find their unique voice and bring about meaningful change in the world.**

Osho emphasized that aloneness is not about withdrawing from society but engaging with it from a place of strength and self-awareness. **When people are comfortable with being alone, they are less likely to conform to societal pressures and more likely to act according to their values and principles.**

Embracing aloneness leads to personal transformation, which, in turn, influences society positively. According to Osho, individuals grounded in their aloneness can inspire others to seek their truth, leading to a collective shift towards a more conscious and enlightened society.

9.5 Creating Personal Norms: Your Aloneness Charter

Osho's teachings often highlighted the importance of creating personal norms and values independent of societal expectations. He believed that aloneness provides the clarity and space necessary for individuals to reflect on what truly matters to them and establish their own living guidelines. **This emphasis on personal norms empowers you so that you regain control of your growth and development.**

In the solitude of aloneness, away from the noise and influence of society, one can listen to the inner voice that speaks of one's true desires and aspirations. Osho encouraged individuals to use this time to contemplate deeply their principles, to decide what is non-negotiable in their lives, and to determine the boundaries that align with their authentic selves.

Creating a personal aloneness charter involves introspection and honesty. It is about defining what aloneness means to you, how you wish to incorporate it into your life, and how it can serve as a foundation for personal growth. This charter is a declaration of independence, a commitment to honoring your need for solitude and the values that emerge from it. Introspection and honesty are vital; I encourage you to engage in self-reflection to develop a sense of personal growth and authenticity.

9.6 Aloneness as a Social Phenomenon: Community and Individuality

Osho's perspective on aloneness extends beyond the individual, encompassing its role as a social phenomenon. He observed that while aloneness is an intrinsic part of our being, it is often overshadowed by the fear of loneliness, a social construct. **According to Osho, loneliness is like darkness; it is an absence of something else, not something that exists independently.** To combat loneliness, one must turn towards the light of aloneness, which is positive and existential.

In society, aloneness is frequently misunderstood and equated with loneliness, leading to a culture where individuals are encouraged to seek constant companionship and activity to avoid facing the enigma they associate with being alone. Osho challenges this notion by suggesting that true aloneness is not about isolation but a deep connection with oneself and, consequently, the larger community.

He proposed that when individuals embrace their aloneness, they can interact with society from a place of strength and authenticity. This new place of interaction can lead to healthier communities where individuals contribute not out of a sense of lack or neediness but from a place of fullness and self-sufficiency.

Chapter 10: Aloneness in Relationships

Aloneness and relationships may seem contradictory, but Osho taught that they are deeply interconnected. This chapter explores how cultivating aloneness can enrich our relationships with others.

10.1 The Paradox of Aloneness and Connection

The Enigma of Solitude

In the intricate dance of human relationships, a profound paradox exists, one that Osho brought to light: The paradox of aloneness and connection. This concept suggests that the foundation of genuine connection with others is not found in the multitude but in the solitude of one's own company.

Self-Companionship as the Key

In the quiet moments of self-reflection, we come to terms with who we are, stripped of the roles and masks we wear in society. Being comfortable in our presence, without the need for external validation, allows us to cultivate a sense of self-sufficiency and inner peace. **This self-companionship, which is the practice of being a friend to oneself, becomes the cornerstone upon which authentic relationships are built.**

Authenticity in Connection

Our interactions become more genuine when approaching others from a place of self-assured solitude. We no longer seek to impress or conform but to understand and be understood. **Our presence becomes a gift of our true self, unadorned and sincere. In this authenticity, we find a deeper level of connection, one that resonates with the core of our being.**

The Impact on Relationships

This paradox has a profound impact on our relationships. It teaches us that the path to profound connections with others winds through the garden of our own solitude. By embracing aloneness, we unlock the ability to be fully present with others, offering the entirety of our attention and compassion. The relationships forged in this manner are not fleeting but are anchored in the bedrock of genuine understanding and mutual respect.

The Universal Lesson

Osho's insight into the paradox of aloneness and connection is a universal lesson. It encourages us to seek solace in solitude, not as a retreat from the world, but as a means to engage with it more fully. **Only when we are comfortable with ourselves can we truly connect with others and the world around us in a meaningful and enriching way.**

Again:

Only when we are comfortable with ourselves can we truly connect with others and the world around us in a meaningful and enriching way.

This exploration reminds us of the intrinsic value of being alone and how it can paradoxically lead us to form more profound and authentic connections with those around us. **This paradoxical idea suggests that by being comfortable with our presence, we can be more present and genuine in our interactions with others.**

10.2 Independence and Interdependence

The Essence of Independence

In the journey of self-discovery, aloneness serves as a profound teacher, imparting the lessons of independence. **This form of autonomy is a fortress of solitude and a pillar of strength.** It is the ability to stand firmly on one's own feet, to make decisions rooted in self-awareness, and to navigate life's currents with an inner compass calibrated by personal values and experiences. This empowerment from aloneness is a source of inspiration and strength, **igniting a fire within us to embrace our individuality.**

Beyond Isolation

True independence is not synonymous with isolation. Instead, it acknowledges that **our individuality is the bedrock upon which we build connections with the world**. It is a state of completeness within oneself, a reservoir of self-esteem and confidence that does not waver in the face of solitude.

The Growth of Interdependence

From this fertile ground of independence, the seeds of interdependence sprout. **Interdependence is recognizing that while we are whole on our own, we are also part of a larger tapestry of human experience.** It is the harmonious exchange between self-reliance and mutual reliance, where the contributions of each individual enhance the collective well-being of the whole; that we evolve and thrive as a species.

Engagement from Fullness

When we engage with others from a place of fullness, our interactions are enriched with the authenticity and richness of our being. **We come not as empty vessels seeking to be filled but as fountains overflowing with the**

waters of our completeness. Our relationships are no longer driven by neediness or scarcity but are instead expressions of our desire to share, give, and grow together from the overflowing of our fullness.

Again:

Our relationships are no longer driven by neediness or scarcity but are instead expressions of our desire to share, give, and grow together from the overflowing of our fullness.

The Symphony of Solitude and Solidarity

The dance between independence and interdependence is a marvelous symphony. It teaches us that aloneness can be a space of empowerment and connection, a celebration of that empowerment. **As we learn to embrace both, we discover that the truest form of connection to others is found in the healthy equilibrium of being able to thrive alone and together.** This symphony is a metaphor for the balance we must strike in our relationships, where we maintain our independence while also valuing and contributing to the collective experience.

Through this exploration, we understand how aloneness can cultivate robust independence, fostering healthy, interdependent relationships. It's a reminder that our individual journeys of growth contribute to the strength and richness of our collective human story. **This independence is not isolation but a strong foundation from which healthy, interdependent relationships can grow.** *We learn to engage with others not out of neediness but from a place of fullness.*

Again:

This independence is not isolation but a strong foundation from which healthy, interdependent relationships can grow. We learn to engage with others not out of neediness but from a place of fullness.

10.3 Authenticity in Relationships

The Journey to Authenticity

In the intricate web of human relationships, authenticity is the foundation that creates the strongest and most beautiful connections. The path to authenticity starts in the private moments of being alone. It's in these solitary moments, away from the pressures of the outside world, where we come face to face with the unfiltered truth of who we are. Authenticity begins from within, in the silent chambers of solitude. It is here that we confront ourselves away from the gaze of others, far from the weight of societal expectations.

Unmasking the Self

As we grow comfortable in our aloneness, we learn to shed the masks and roles society often imposes upon us. **The need for approval or validation recedes, and we stand in the light of our self-acceptance**. This self-assurance, rooted in our acceptance of who we truly are, allows us to present our true selves to others, not as characters in a play seeking applause but as genuine individuals sharing our reality.

Deepening Connections

When we approach relationships from this place of authenticity, we invite deeper intimacy and understanding. Our interactions are no longer superficial exchanges but become rich dialogues of shared truths and mutual respect. **We offer not just our presence but our essence**; in doing so, we foster more profound and fulfilling connections.

The Fulfillment of Being Seen

In embracing authentic relationships, we experience the fulfillment of being seen for who we truly are. The joy of such connections lies not in the quantity but in the quality and depth of the bonds formed. **These relationships are built on trust and openness, where each person is valued for their individuality**

and not for the roles they play. This sense of being valued and appreciated is critical to authentic relationships, making us feel deeply cherished and understood.

A Ripple Effect of Authenticity

The authenticity we cultivate in our relationships extends beyond our personal sphere. It inspires others to embrace their truth, creating a ripple effect that transforms the fabric of our communities. As more individuals choose to live authentically, we move towards a society where genuine connections are the norm, not the exception. This potential for positive change and transformation is a powerful aspect of authenticity.

Through this exploration, we are reminded of the power of aloneness to foster independence, which enriches our relationships with authenticity and depth. **It's a testament to the idea that by being true to ourselves, we can create more meaningful and satisfying connections with others. When we are comfortable with aloneness, we bring our true selves to our relationships.** We are less likely to wear masks or play roles because we are not seeking approval or validation. Our relationships then become more genuine and fulfilling.

10.4 Empathy and Compassion

The Introspective Solitude

In the quietude of aloneness, we embark on an introspective journey that takes us through the unexplored territories of our inner landscape. In these moments of solitude, we come face to face with our shadows, the parts of ourselves that we often hide or deny. This confrontation is not one of conflict but of reconciliation.

Confronting and Accepting Imperfections

As we learn to sit with our imperfections, we cultivate a sense of self-compassion. We begin to understand that our flaws are not failings but facets of our humanity. This acceptance softens the harshness we often judge ourselves and opens the door to a more forgiving and compassionate view of our nature. **By being more forgiving and compassionate to ourselves, we can be more forgiving and compassionate to others.**

Again:

By being more forgiving and compassionate to ourselves, we can be more forgiving and compassionate to others.

The Emergence of Empathy

This **self-compassion** naturally extends outward, transforming into empathy for others. When we recognize our vulnerabilities, we become more attuned to the struggles and sufferings of those around us. **Our hearts, having been tenderized by our own experiences, resonate with the pains and joys of others.**

Kindness as a Universal Language

Empathy blossoms into acts of kindness, a universal language that transcends barriers and connects us at a fundamental level. **Our interactions become imbued with a gentleness born of the understanding that everyone is fighting their battles, often invisible to the naked eye.**

The Ripple Effect of Compassion

The compassion we nurture within ourselves creates a ripple effect, influencing our relationships and communities. It becomes a beacon that guides our actions and interactions, fostering an environment where understanding and kindness are not exceptions but the norm.

This exploration reminds us of the transformative power of aloneness in developing empathy and compassion. **In solitude, we confront our shadows and learn to accept our imperfections. This self-compassion translates into greater understanding and kindness towards others**. It teaches us that by embracing our humanity, we can extend a hand of solidarity to others, creating a world that is a little more understanding and kind.

Let me say that one more time:

In solitude, we confront our shadows and learn to accept our imperfections. This self-compassion translates into greater understanding and kindness towards others.

10.5 Balancing Aloneness and Social Life

Balancing aloneness and social life is an art that requires mindful practice and intention. Here are some insights and additional points to consider:

Scheduling Alone Time

Just as we meticulously plan gatherings and outings with friends and family, carving out moments for solitude is crucial. **Carving out moments for solitude for ourselves isn't merely a luxury but a necessity for our mental and emotional well-being.** By scheduling alone time, we create a sanctuary in our busy lives where we can reconnect with our inner selves, reflect on our experiences, and nurture our passions. This balance is the key to maintaining a healthy sense of self amidst the demands of social interactions.

Communicating Your Needs

Openness with loved ones about the value of solitude in your life is essential. Communicate your needs clearly and compassionately, explaining that these periods of aloneness are not a rejection of their company but a way to rejuvenate your spirit. When others understand that your well-being thrives on this balance, they are more likely to offer support and respect your boundaries.

Cultivating Shared Aloneness

Shared aloneness is a beautiful concept where two or more individuals engage in separate activities in each other's presence, enjoying solitude without isolation. Whether reading in the same room or painting in shared silence, cultivate shared aloneness to maintain a connection with others while honoring your personal space.

Embracing Quality Over Quantity

In social interactions, focus on the quality of connections rather than the quantity. Meaningful conversations and experiences with a close friend can be more fulfilling than a large gathering where superficial exchanges prevail. Prioritize relationships that enrich your life and align with your values.

Finding Solitude in Nature

Nature has a unique way of offering solitude, even in its vastness. Spend time outdoors, whether it's a walk in the park or a hike in the wilderness. The natural world provides a backdrop for introspection and a break from the human-made world, allowing you to recharge in its tranquil beauty.

Setting Boundaries

Learn to say 'No' when social obligations conflict with your need for solitude. Setting boundaries is not selfish; it's a form of self-care. Honoring your limits ensures you don't deplete your energy and can show up as your best self in both solitary and social settings.

Again:

Learn to say 'No' when social obligations conflict with your need for solitude. Setting boundaries is not selfish; it's a form of self-care.

Integrating Mindfulness Practices

Incorporate mindfulness practices into your daily routine. Meditation, yoga, or simply a few minutes of deep breathing can create pockets of solitude and peace in your day, helping you stay centered amid a busy social life.

By embracing these practices, you can find a harmonious balance between the enriching experience of solitude and the joy of social life. **Remember, it's not about isolating yourself but about nurturing a relationship with yourself that, in turn, enhances your relationships with others.**

10.6 Practical Application of Aloneness: Daily Life Integration

Osho's teachings on aloneness are not just philosophical concepts but practical tools that can be integrated into everyday life. He believed that aloneness should be a living experience woven into the fabric of our daily routines. The practice of aloneness is about finding moments of solitude amidst the chaos of life, where one can reconnect with one's inner self and the flow of existence.

To integrate aloneness into daily life, Osho suggested simple yet profound practices:

Mindful Mornings: Start the day with a few moments of silence, sitting alone, simply observing the body's breath and sensations. Simply observing the body's breath and sensations sets a mindfulness tone for the day ahead.

Alone Time Blocks: Schedule short blocks of time dedicated to being alone throughout the day. During these periods, engage in activities that nourish the soul, such as reading, meditating, or simply being in nature.

Conscious Commuting: Use commuting time as an opportunity for aloneness. Instead of filling the space with distractions, turn inward and use the journey for reflection and contemplation.

Solo Lunches: Take occasional solo lunches as a break from social interactions. Use this time to enjoy the food mindfully and appreciate the eating experience.

Evening Wind-Down: End the day by disconnecting from electronic devices and spending time alone, journaling, or planning for the next day in solitude.

By incorporating these practices into daily life, aloneness becomes a source of strength and clarity. Osho's teachings encourage us to embrace these moments of solitude as opportunities for self-discovery and inner peace.

10.7 How Aloneness Can Strengthen Romantic Relationships

Osho's teachings suggest that aloneness can significantly enhance the quality of our relationships. **He believed that when individuals are comfortable with being alone, they bring a sense of wholeness and self-sufficiency to their interactions.** This wholeness allows for healthier and more fulfilling relationships, as each person is not looking to the other to fill a void but rather to share in the joy of their completeness. This is very important, and 99% of people ignore this, which leads to unnecessary heartache. When you are comfortable being alone, you exude a sense of completeness. You can align with a deep joy within, a joy coming from the Source within. This sense of completeness allows for healthier and more fulfilling relationships because now, each person is not looking to the other to fill a void but rather to share in the joy of their completeness. **My joy is overflowing, and I am looking for someone capable of sharing my joy.**

According to Osho, aloneness is the foundation upon which true love can grow. When individuals are alone, they can discover their depths, enabling them to appreciate the depths in others. **This deep appreciation fosters a genuine connection that is not based on dependency or neediness but on mutual recognition of each other's fullness.**

Osho emphasized that aloneness should not be confused with isolation. While isolation is separation from others, aloneness is a state of being that enhances one's capacity to love and be loved. **In the space of aloneness, one can learn the art of listening, understanding, and compassion—qualities essential for meaningful relationships.**

10.8 Setting Personal Boundaries: The Interplay with Aloneness

Osho's teachings on aloneness often touched upon the importance of setting personal boundaries. **He believed understanding and respecting one's boundaries is essential for maintaining a healthy state of aloneness.** These boundaries are not barriers to keeping others out but a declaration of self-respect and an acknowledgment of personal space and needs.

Setting personal boundaries involves recognizing where one ends and another begins. It's about understanding one's limits and communicating them clearly to others. Osho taught that when individuals honor their boundaries, they can engage with others more authentically without losing themselves in the process.

According to Osho, aloneness is enriched by the presence of boundaries. They allow individuals to retreat into their solitude when needed, to recharge and connect with their inner selves. This practice of retreating and returning can lead to more dynamic and fulfilling interactions with others, as one comes from a place of fullness rather than emptiness.

10.9 Setting Boundaries: Healthy Separateness in Close Bonds

Establishing and maintaining personal boundaries is crucial for nurturing aloneness and ensuring it is a source of strength and self-discovery. Drawing from Osho's philosophy, here are practical ways to assert these boundaries across various aspects of life:

Work

- **Prioritize Your Tasks:** Start by identifying your most important tasks and allocate specific times to focus on them without interruptions.
- **Communicate Your Needs:** Clearly communicate your need for uninterrupted work time to colleagues and superiors.
- **Set Physical Boundaries:** Create a physical workspace that signals to others that you are in a concentration zone.

- **Use Technology Wisely:** Utilize tools like email auto-responders or messaging status options to inform others when you are not immediately available.

Relationships

- **Express Your Needs:** Have open and honest conversations with loved ones about your need for alone time.
- **Schedule Alone Time:** Just as you would schedule a date or family time, schedule time for yourself and treat it with the same importance.
- **Respect Others' Boundaries:** By respecting others' needs for space, you set a precedent for your own boundaries to be respected.
- **Balance Togetherness and Separateness:** Find activities you can do alone that also contribute to the relationship, like reading a book you can later discuss.

Social Settings

- **Plan Your Social Calendar:** Be selective about social engagements, ensuring you have enough alone time before and after events.
- **Learn to Say No:** Politely declining invitations when you need alone time is a healthy practice.
- **Take Breaks During Events:** If you're at a social event and feel overwhelmed, stepping away for a few minutes is okay to recharge.

General Tips

- **Self-Awareness:** Regularly check in with yourself to understand your current needs for aloneness.
- **Assertiveness:** Communicate your boundaries assertively but kindly without feeling guilty for prioritizing your well-being.
- **Consistency:** Be consistent in enforcing your boundaries, as this helps others understand and respect your needs over time.

- **Flexibility:** While maintaining boundaries, be flexible enough to adjust them as needed based on life's changing circumstances.

Osho's philosophy emphasizes the importance of aloneness in discovering one's true nature. **Setting and maintaining personal boundaries creates the necessary space to delve into self-exploration and growth.** These boundaries are not walls but rather the defining lines that allow you to flourish both in solitude and the company of others, leading to a more authentic and fulfilling life. **Remember, aloneness is not loneliness; it's a fertile ground for creativity, introspection, and personal evolution.**

10.10 Alone Together: Engaging in Parallel Activities

Osho's teachings on aloneness often emphasize its role as a tool for self-empowerment and claiming personal sovereignty. **He believed that aloneness is not a state of deficiency but a state of completeness, where an individual can access their innate power and wisdom.** According to Osho, when one is alone, one is in the company of the whole universe, and in this space, one can find the strength to be one's master.

Aloneness allows individuals to step back from societal pressures and expectations, listen to their needs and desires, and make decisions based on their true selves. It is a space where one can cultivate self-reliance and confidence, free from the influence of others.

Osho taught that personal sovereignty is taking responsibility for one's life, thoughts, and actions. It is about living by one's values and truths rather than conforming to external standards. Aloneness provides the clarity and solitude necessary for this level of introspection and self-governance.

10.11 From Dependency to Interdependence: Transition Stories

The steps from dependency to interdependence are delicate and profound in the dance of relationships. Imagine a garden where two trees stand side by side, their roots entwined beneath the soil. Their roots entwined beneath the soil is the story of interdependence—a tale not of two souls lost in each other's shadows but of individuals basking in their sunlight while contributing to a shared canopy.

Aloneness, often misunderstood, is the soil from which the seed of interdependence sprouts. It is the stillness where the soul whispers to the self, nurturing an inner sanctuary that blooms outward, touching the heart of another without clinging. **In the embrace of solitude, we discover the strength to stand alone—not in isolation, but in the richness of our being, offering to our partners not a half seeking wholeness but a whole engaging in unity.**

Again:

In the embrace of solitude, we discover the strength to stand alone—not in isolation, but in the richness of our being, offering to our partners not a half seeking wholeness but a whole engaging in unity.

The journey from dependency is marked by stories as varied as the stars. Consider the tale of Maya and Antoine, whose love once resembled a vine clinging to a sturdy oak. In time, they learned to cherish their separate moments of solitude—Maya finding solace in her poetry, Antoine in his long, reflective walks. As they cultivated their inner gardens, their relationship transformed. **No longer the vine and the oak, but two oaks standing tall, their individual strengths fortifying their bond.**

One must embrace practices that honor the self and the union to walk this path. Setting aside time for personal growth becomes a sacred ritual, not retreating from the relationship but advancing towards a deeper connection. **Encouraging each other's pursuits, they become cheerleaders of dreams and architects of a shared vision where personal aspirations are not competitors but co-creators of their collective story. You become co-creators of your collective story.**

Yet, the path is not without its brambles. The fear of growing apart and the pang of misunderstood needs are the trials on the road to interdependence. But with each challenge comes a beacon of solutions: communication as clear as a mountain stream, boundaries as respected as ancient stones, **and the understanding that being alone together is an art, a parallel play of spirits**

in harmony.

Ultimately, the narrative of aloneness within relationships is a mosaic of transformation tales. It is a testament to the power of solitude to not only coexist with intimacy but to deepen its roots, allowing us to stand together, not as halves, but as wholes—**interdependent, strong, and beautifully alone together.**

Chapter 11: Addressing Generational Views on Aloneness

11.1 Baby Boomers: Rediscovering Self After Retirement

As the golden sun of retirement dawns on the horizon for the Baby Boomer generation, a new chapter of self-discovery beckons. **Retirement is a time of reflection, a period where the hustle of career and the chorus of familial obligations fade into a quietude ripe with boundless possibility and the freedom to explore.**

Rediscovery is the heart of this journey. It's a passage marked by the wisdom of years and the freedom to explore the inner landscapes often left uncharted due to life's incessant demands. **Aloneness in this season is not a void but a vast canvas, waiting for the vibrant colors of latent passions and unfulfilled dreams.**

For many Boomers, solitude becomes a cherished ally, a source of joy and fulfillment. In the stillness of their own company, they reconnect with the youthful aspirations that once sparked their spirits. **The painter's brush, the writer's pen, and the gardener's spade become instruments of joy, tools for crafting a life of authenticity and joy.**

Yet, this aloneness is not without its challenges. The transition from a life defined by work to leisure can stir a disruption of identity and purpose. Here, the wisdom of Osho serves as a lighthouse, guiding the wayward sailor to a safe harbor. His teachings on aloneness remind us that within each individual lies an ocean of potential, waiting to be navigated with courage and curiosity.

In embracing solitude, the Baby Boomers find not loneliness but a rekindling of the self—a renaissance of spirit that illuminates the twilight years with the glow of inner peace and the warmth of newfound freedom.

11.2 Gen X: Balancing Career, Family, and Self-Time

Generation X, at the crossroads of progress and tradition, grapples with a distinct set of challenges. **Their daily juggling is a delicate balance between career, family, and the precious temple of self-time.**

Gen X, the bridge generation, carries the torch of technological revolution while holding onto the threads of traditional values. **They are the silent warriors, often overlooked, yet their battles are fought in the quiet corners of early mornings and late nights, where the only audience is the echo of their thoughts.**

Aloneness for this generation is a rare gem, hard-earned and precious. In these moments of solitude, they find the strength to juggle the myriad roles demanded by the modern world. **Aloneness is not a retreat but a strategic advance into the depths of their being, where they can recharge, reflect, and emerge with renewed vigor.**

For the Gen Xers, the art of aloneness is not about escapism but finding equilibrium. It's a dance of introspection, where every step, every moment alone, is a step towards inner harmony. **In the stillness, they craft their legacy, weaving the wisdom of experience with the freshness of innovation.**

The teachings of Osho resonate deeply with this generation as they seek to find authenticity in a world that often values appearance over essence. **His insights on aloneness offer a compass to navigate the complex waters of mid-life, guiding them towards a harbor where the only expectation to meet is the one they set for themselves.**

In the embrace of aloneness, Gen X redefines success. It's no longer about the accolades or the accumulation of wealth but about the richness of a life well-lived, balanced, and true to one's rhythm.

11.3 Millennials: Aloneness in the Age of Social Media

In the digital era's relentless stream, Millennials navigate the rapids with a unique blend of connectedness and isolation. Born into a world where virtual interactions often eclipse physical ones, they stand at the vanguard of a new paradigm of aloneness.

Millennials, the digital natives, have crafted a mosaic of identities, each pixelated avatar a facet of their complex realities. Their aloneness is a paradox, one where the crowd is ever-present, yet the individual can feel profoundly solitary amidst the online multitudes.

The art of aloneness for this generation is a dance with duality. It is the quest to find silence in the cacophony of notifications, to carve out a space for introspection in the exhibition halls of social media. **In their solitude, they seek authenticity, a voice that resonates with truth beyond the curated galleries of their digital personas.**

Osho's teachings offer clarity in the fog of constant connectivity. His wisdom on aloneness challenges the Millennial to disconnect, turn inward, and discover the richness that lies beyond the 'like' buttons and the 'share' icons.

Again:

Osho's teachings offer clarity in the fog of constant connectivity. His wisdom on aloneness challenges the Millennial to disconnect, turn inward, and discover the richness that lies beyond the 'like' buttons and the 'share' icons.

It is an invitation to a journey within, to a place where the self is not a profile to be scrolled past but a universe to be explored.

For the Millennial, aloneness becomes an act of rebellion, a statement of intent. It is the choice to pause the endless feed, mute the world, and listen to the rhythm of their heartbeat. **In this sacred space, they find not loneliness but a connection to the self, the truest form of social networking.**

11.4 Gen Z: Redefining Identity and Success in Solitude

Generation Z forges a path less trodden in the quiet corners of a world loud with ambition and display. **They are the architects of a new solitude, where aloneness is not a byproduct of circumstance but a chosen companion on the journey to self-definition.**

Gen Z, the inheritors of a digital legacy, are acutely aware of the noise that permeates every aspect of modern existence. Yet, in their aloneness, they find a sanctuary where the chatter fades and the voice within gains clarity. **In the embrace of solitude, it is here that they redefine what it means to be successful.**

Success, for this generation, is not measured in milestones or accolades but in the authenticity of one's narrative. Aloneness becomes the crucible in which identity is forged, away from the gaze of peers and the expectations of predecessors. **It is a space of creation where the self is sculpted not from the clay of societal norms but from the raw materials of personal truth and aspiration.**

The teachings of Osho resonate with Gen Z's intuitive understanding of aloneness as a gateway to inner freedom. His insights offer a map to navigate the labyrinth of the self, encouraging a departure from the collective script to author a story of individual essence.

In solitude, Gen Z discovers the power of introspection and the beauty of an unshared moment. They learn that in the silence of being alone, one can hear the whispers of a future being born, a future where success is a personal revolution, a quiet triumph of the spirit.

11.5 Cross-Generational Dialogues on Aloneness

In the grand theater of time, where generations share the stage, a conversation unfolds—a dialogue rich with the wisdom of ages and the freshness of youth. This grand theater of time is the symposium of solitude, where Baby Boomers, Gen X, Millennials, and Gen Z gather to exchange their insights on aloneness.

Cross-generational dialogues are the threads that weave the tapestry of understanding. Each generation brings its unique experiences of solitude, painting a picture that spans the spectrum of human emotion and thought. The Baby Boomers speak of aloneness as a newfound friend in the autumn of life, while Gen X discusses the balancing act of solitude amidst life's full bloom.

Millennials, with their digital lexicon, share tales of disconnecting to connect with the self, and Gen Z, bold and unbridled, champions the cause of aloneness as the crucible of identity. **Together, they explore the multifaceted nature of solitude, learning from each other, challenging preconceived notions, and building bridges across the generational divide.**

These dialogues are not mere exchanges of words but a collective journey toward a deeper understanding of aloneness. They are a testament to the timeless quest for self-discovery that transcends age and era. In sharing stories, laughter, and tears, a common truth emerges: aloneness is not a condition to be feared but a state to be cherished, a universal experience that binds the human spirit across the time continuum.

11.6 Bridging the Gap: Learning Aloneness Across Ages

As the chapters of history turn, each generation inscribes its legacy of solitude. The wisdom of aloneness, a timeless mentor, speaks to every age in the language of the heart. A lesson resonates across the generational divide in the shared classroom of existence: the art of being alone is a universal curriculum, an education in the essence of being.

Bridging the gap between generations is an act of collective introspection. It is an acknowledgment that, despite the differences in upbringing, technology, and social norms, the need for aloneness is a common thread that weaves through human experience. **With their rich reservoirs of life lessons, Baby Boomers offer a perspective of aloneness from someone who has already made a long and enriching journey. Gen X, nestled between the old and the new, shares the wisdom of balance, where solitude is a refuge and a springboard for life's myriad roles.**

Millennials, ever-connected yet often alone, bring the paradox of their

existence to the table, where aloneness is both a challenge and a cherished escape. Gen Z, bold in their quest for authenticity, views solitude as the crucible of self-definition, a space where the world's noise dims and the inner voice gains volume.

In this cross-generational dialogue, the learning is bidirectional. The younger learn from the elder's experiences, drawing strength from their trials and triumphs. In turn, the older generations find renewal in the fresh perspectives of youth, discovering that the journey of aloneness is ever-evolving, ever-unfolding.

Together, they build a bridge of understanding, a structure strong enough to carry the weight of shared solitude. It is a bridge that spans time, a testament to the enduring nature of aloneness as a facet of the human condition. Through this shared learning, the gap narrows, and the path of aloneness becomes a shared journey, a collective voyage toward the horizon of self-discovery.

Chapter 12: Advanced Spiritual Insights and Practices

12.1 Advanced Meditation Techniques for Deep Solitude

The soul's whispers echo with clarity in the sacred silence of solitude. For those who venture deeper into the realm of aloneness, advanced meditation techniques await, serving as vessels to navigate the inner cosmos.

Advanced meditation is a transformative odyssey, a journey beyond the surface calm into the profound depths where the essence of being resides. It is here, in the deep solitude of meditation, that one encounters the boundless expanse of the self—a universe within, infinite and serene.

The techniques are varied, each a key to unlocking different doors within. There is the **Vipassana**, the art of seeing things as they truly are, a practice of profound insight and purity of vision. The **Zazen**, a Zen Buddhist method, invites stillness and presence, a return to the very core of existence. And then there is the **Transcendental Meditation**, a journey beyond thought, where the mantra becomes a raft on the river of consciousness.

These practices are not for the faint of heart. They require dedication, a yearning for truth, and the courage to face the self in its rawest form. The journey may be challenging, with moments of doubt and discomfort. But for those who persevere, the rewards are immeasurable. **In the depths of solitude, one finds a connection to all things, a unity that transcends the illusion of**

separation.

Osho's insights into these advanced techniques offer a guiding light. His teachings, profound yet accessible, serve as a map for the seeker. He speaks of meditation not as an escape but as an embrace—a loving acceptance of the present moment, a celebration of life in its entirety.

In embracing advanced meditation, the practitioner discovers solitude and communion with the universal spirit. It is a dance of the individual flame with the eternal fire, merging the drop with the ocean.

12.2 Spiritual Awakening Through Aloneness

In the quietude of aloneness, there lies a path less traveled, winding through the inner wilderness where the seeds of spiritual awakening are sown. It is an inward journey where the noise of the external world fades into a hushed reverence for the soul's unfolding.

Spiritual awakening is the blossoming of awareness, a delicate unfurling of the petals of perception. In the solitude of this sacred space, the veils of illusion lift, and the light of truth bathes the seeker in its radiant glow.

The process is transformative, a metamorphosis from the cocoon of conditioned existence to the freedom of spiritual flight. It is in the embrace of aloneness that one discovers the interconnectedness of all beings, the thread of consciousness that weaves through every heart and soul. This awakening is not a sudden event, but a gradual unfolding, a journey of self-discovery and self-realization that leads to a profound shift in perception and understanding.

Osho's teachings serve as a lantern in the dark woods of the seeker's quest. Like a gentle hand on the shoulder, his words guide the wayward traveler back to the road of self-realization. **He speaks of aloneness as the fertile ground from which the lotus of enlightenment emerges, rooted in the mud of the material world yet reaching for the heavens.**

In this aloneness, the seeker finds solace and strength. **The journey is one of paradoxes—where solitude leads to unity, silence speaks volumes, and emptiness is filled with the infinite.** It is a pilgrimage to the core of one's being, where the discovery of the self is the discovery of the divine.

12.3 Integrating Aloneness into Daily Spiritual Practices - Stitching the Sacred into the Mundane

In the tapestry of daily life, aloneness is woven into the fabric of spiritual practice, a golden thread that adds depth and texture to the seeker's journey. **In the quiet moments of each day, the practice of aloneness becomes a living meditation, a continuous thread of awareness that stitches the sacred into the mundane.**

Daily spiritual practices are the loom upon which the fabric of enlightenment is crafted. Each thread of solitude, each solitary moment, is an opportunity to weave consciousness into every action. **Aloneness infuses each moment with intention and presence, whether it's in the early morning stillness, the pause between tasks, or the reflective silence of the night.**

Again:

Aloneness infuses each moment with intention and presence, whether it's in the early morning stillness, the pause between tasks, or the reflective silence of the night.

The integration of aloneness into daily life is an art, a delicate balance of engagement and retreat. It is the conscious choice to step back from the outer world and step into the inner sanctum, even if just for a breath, a heartbeat, a fleeting instant. **Whether it's taking a solitary walk in nature, enjoying a quiet cup of tea, or simply pausing to breathe deeply, in these moments, the seeker finds a refuge, a wellspring of peace that refreshes the spirit and nourishes the soul.**

Osho's vision of spirituality is not escapism but an immersive presence. He teaches that genuine spiritual practice is not confined to the cushion or the temple but is alive in every breath, every step, and every solitary beat of the heart. **Aloneness is not a separate practice but an integral part of the spiritual fabric, a sacred quality that permeates every aspect of life.**

In embracing daily aloneness, the spiritual seeker discovers the extraor-

dinary within the ordinary. Seemingly mundane acts – sipping tea, the rhythmic motion of walking, the silent observation of a blooming flower, watching the sunset, etc. – become a meditation, a silent prayer of gratitude for the miracle of existence.

12.4 Osho's Techniques for Experiencing Universal Connection

In the solitude of the self lies a bridge to the cosmos, a connection that transcends the physical and touches the essence of all existence. Osho's techniques for experiencing this universal connection are keys that unlock the doors to a realm where the individual and the infinite converge.

Meditative Techniques: Osho's meditative practices are invitations to journey beyond the ego to a place where the self dissolves into the vastness of the universe. Techniques like **Dynamic Meditation** and **Kundalini Meditation** are transformative processes that shake the foundations of the isolated self, stirring the energy that connects us to the whole.

Nature and Existence: Osho encourages seekers to commune with nature and see themselves reflected in the rivers, mountains, and skies. In the aloneness of nature, one finds a mirror for the soul, a reflection of the universal dance of creation.

Love and Compassion: Through practices of love and compassion, Osho guides individuals to open their hearts to the world. **In the space of aloneness, love becomes not a transaction but a state of being, a radiance that illuminates the interconnectedness of life.**

Celebration of Life: Osho's vision of spirituality is one of joyous celebration, where each moment is an opportunity to honor the divine play of existence. **Aloneness is not a somber affair but a joyful embrace of life's myriad expressions.**

In practicing these techniques, the seeker finds that aloneness is the ultimate connection. **In the quietness of being alone, the symphony of the universe is heard most clearly, a melody that sings of oneness, a chorus that celebrates the unity of all.**

12.5 Overcoming Spiritual Loneliness: Finding Unity in Aloneness

In the seeker's journey, there comes a time when the path narrows, and the companions dwindle, leaving one to walk the road of spiritual pursuit in solitude. **This passage, often tinged with the hues of loneliness, is not a detour but a vital stretch of the voyage toward enlightenment.**

Spiritual loneliness is a paradoxical companion. It whispers of isolation yet speaks the truth of oneness. In the depths of this seeming solitude, the seeker is invited to confront the illusion of separation, to peel back the layers of the self until nothing remains but the essence of unity with all existence.

The challenge is to transform loneliness into a profound aloneness rich with presence. It is a process of shedding the need for external validation and turning inward, where the world's din softens, and the inner dialogue becomes a monologue of the soul.

Again:

It is a process of shedding the need for external validation and turning inward, where the world's din softens, and the inner dialogue becomes a monologue of the soul.

Osho's guidance shines like a beacon for those navigating the waters of spiritual loneliness. **He teaches that true aloneness is not a state of lack but fullness. In aloneness, one is not empty but overflowing with the totality of being.** It is a space where the individual merges with the universal, **where the drop becomes the ocean.**

Through meditation, mindfulness, and the embrace of nature, the seeker learns to find comfort in the discomfort of solitude. **The practice becomes not just a method but a way of life, a continuous affirmation of the interconnectedness that binds every atom of the universe.**

In overcoming spiritual loneliness, the seeker discovers a hidden treasure—a sense of unity that cannot be disturbed by the comings and goings of life. **It is a realization that we are never truly alone, for we are eternally connected to the infinite web of life, a part of the cosmic dance that is both the journey and the destination.**

12.6 Embracing Aloneness as a Continuous Journey

The path of aloneness is not a destination but a journey—a perpetual pilgrimage through the landscapes of the self and the spirit. It is a voyage that unfolds with each breath, each moment of solitude, each silent communion with the essence of existence.

Aloneness as a Journey: This journey is one of constant discovery, where each step reveals new horizons within the heart and the mind. It is a passage marked not by milestones but by the evolution of consciousness, a deepening of the connection with the self and the divine.

The Eternal Seeker: The seeker on this path is an eternal traveler who understands that the quest for enlightenment is not a race but a walk in the garden of wisdom. With each experience of aloneness, the seeker gathers insights like flowers, weaving them into a garland of understanding that adorns the soul.

Living Meditation: Osho teaches that aloneness is a living meditation, a practice that does not begin or end but flows like a river through the landscape of life. It is an art of being present with oneself, listening to the whispers of the inner voice, and honoring the sacredness of solitary moments.

The Dance of Solitude: In the dance of solitude, the seeker learns the steps of self-love, self-acceptance, and self-transcendence. It is a dance that requires no audience, for the music is the rhythm of the universe itself, and the dance floor is the vast expanse of the seeker's being.

Continuous Transformation: The beauty of this journey is in its constant transformation. Aloneness is not a static state but a dynamic process of becoming a never-ending metamorphosis. With each cycle of solitude, the seeker sheds old skin, emerging renewed and closer to the core of true self.

In embracing aloneness as a continuous journey, the seeker finds that the path is lined with the treasures of insight, peace, and an unshakeable connection to all that is. It is a journey that has no end, for it is woven into the very fabric of existence—a journey that is as eternal as the spirit that embarks upon it.

Chapter 13: The Creative Power of Aloneness

In Chapter 13, we explore the profound influence of aloneness on the creative process. Aloneness is a force that has sparked significant artistic and intellectual breakthroughs throughout history.

13.1 The Solitude of Great Minds

History is a tapestry woven with tales of creators who embraced aloneness to kindle their creative fires. Writers, artists, scientists, and thinkers have all discovered an inexhaustible source of inspiration in aloneness. We remember the lives of great minds like Isaac Newton, who formulated the laws of motion in the seclusion of the Great Plague, and Virginia Woolf, who championed the necessity of "a room of one's own" for creation. In the sacred silence of history, the solitude of great minds resonates with the echoes of genius. **Within the serene cloisters of aloneness, the brightest ideas take flight, where thoughts unfurl their wings, and the imagination ascends to celestial heights.**

In the profound stillness of their solitude, visionaries like Nikola Tesla and Walter Russell engaged in a silent discourse with the enigmas of the cosmos. Artists such as Claude Monet and Wolfgang Amadeus Mozart reached into the ethereal, translating the silent language of solitude into timeless masterpieces that stir the soul. Their aloneness served as a crucible, a hallowed space where the alchemy of creativity transmuted the leaden quietude into golden insights, igniting the torch of inspiration for future generations.

13.2 The Space to Create

Aloneness carves out the physical and mental expanse essential for flowering creativity. **Ideas can incubate and take shape in the tranquil interludes, distanced from the clamor of the world.** This section will explore strategies to cultivate and safeguard this hallowed space daily.

The Silence That Speaks

In the hush of aloneness, the **inner voice** emerges with clarity. How do you attune to this inner voice and trust this inner guide? This **inner voice** navigates the creative journey and often possesses wisdom beyond our conscious grasp. I will mention again the steps outlined in previous Chapters. Redundancy allows for deeper insight integration.

   1. Establish a Daily Solitude Practice:

   - Set aside a specific time each day for solitude. Early morning or late evening can be ideal times when the world is quieter.

   - Find a comfortable and private space where you won't be disturbed.

   2. Minimize Distractions:

   - Turn off electronic devices or silence them to avoid interruptions.

   - Inform others of your aloneness practice to ensure they respect this time.

   3. Engage in Mindfulness or Meditation:

   - Begin your aloneness practice with a few minutes of mindfulness or meditation to center yourself.

   - Focus on your breath to help quiet the mind and bring your attention to the present moment.

   4. Listen Actively:

   - Pay attention to the thoughts and feelings that arise. Don't judge or dismiss them; observe.

   - Keep a journal nearby to jot down insights or ideas that come to you.

   5. Dialogue with Your Inner Voice:

- Ask yourself questions about your creative work and listen for the responses from within.

- Be open to the answers, even if they're unexpected or lead you in a new direction.

6. Practice Patience:

- Understand that connecting with your inner voice can take time and may take time.

- Be patient with yourself and the process, allowing your inner wisdom to surface in time.

7. Trust and Take Action:

- When you receive guidance from your inner voice, trust it.

- Take small steps to act on the insights you gain, reinforcing your trust in your inner voice.

8. Reflect on Your Experiences:

- At the end of your aloneness practice, reflect on what you've learned or discovered.

- Consider how you can apply this knowledge to your creative endeavors.

By incorporating these steps into your routine, you can cultivate a deeper connection with your **inner voice** and harness its wisdom to enhance your creative journey. Remember, the key is consistency and openness to the insights that solitude can bring.

Flow and Focus: The Symphony of Solitude

In the sacred enclave of aloneness, a symphony of silence orchestrates a state of flow, where the relentless march of time softens to a gentle cadence, and the creator becomes one with their art. **Aloneness is not a mere absence but a sanctuary of boundless creativity, where the spirit is liberated from the fetters of the mundane.** The quietude speaks in a language without words, articulating the rhythm of flow and focus that emerges when the cacophony of the world fades into a distant murmur, leaving the creator cradled in a cosmos of infinite possibilities, infused with a profound sense of empowerment and liberation.

Within this hallowed embrace of solitude, the writer unearths the elusive words that have danced just beyond reach, and the painter beholds the spectrum of colors that have slumbered unseen within the mind's vast palette. It is a domain where the chains of creative blockages melt away, where the muse descends, whispering secrets intimately to the artist's soul. Here, in the revered hush, the canvas of creation stretches to the horizons, and the potential for innovation knows no bounds, igniting a blaze of passion and anticipation for the wonders yet to unfold.

The Alchemy of Creation

Each moment becomes an alchemy process in aloneness, transmuting the lead of uncertainty into the gold of clarity. The artist's hands move with a precision born of a mind in perfect harmony with its purpose. The words flow from the pen, the brushstrokes from the palette, each a testament to the transformative power of aloneness in the creative process.

The Dance of Ideas

Ideas pirouette through the stillness, each a spark that could light up new worlds. In their solitary dance, the creator partners with inspiration, moving to a rhythm that only the heart can hear. It is a dance that weaves the fabric of dreams into the tapestry of reality.

The Oasis of Innovation

Aloneness is the oasis in the desert of distraction, where the wellspring of originality bubbles forth, clear and sweet. It is here that the creator drinks deeply, quenching a thirst for the novel and the groundbreaking. Each sip is a promise of future masterpieces, each gulp a draught of the yet-to-be-discovered, igniting a blaze of passion and anticipation for the wonders yet to unfold.

Overcoming Creative Blocks

Aloneness can be a formidable ally in surmounting creative obstacles. By eliminating external diversions and devising pathways to transcend them, we can face our internal barriers. This section will offer tactics for harnessing aloneness to overcome creative blocks and ascend to unprecedented heights of creativity.

Overcoming Creative Blocks: The Journey Through Aloneness

Aloneness is a sentinel at the gates of creativity, a formidable ally in overcoming the daunting specters of creative blocks. Within the sanctum of seclusion, we can confront our internal barriers, those silent adversaries that stifle the flow of inspiration. By stripping away the cacophony of external diversions, we create a crucible for transformation, where the raw materials of our imagination can be refined and shaped into expressions of our most profound insights.

The Labyrinth of the Mind

Venturing into the labyrinth of our minds can be an intimidating odyssey. Yet, it is a necessary pilgrimage to unearth the treasures buried beneath layers of doubt and hesitation. Solitude offers the keys to this inner realm, inviting us to navigate its complex corridors with introspection and courage.

Strategies for Embracing Aloneness

Embrace the Quietude

- Seek the quiet corners of your world, where the whispers of your inner muse can be heard above the din of daily life.

- Let the silence envelop you, becoming a canvas upon which your thoughts can freely paint their stories.

Confront the Void

- In the absence of noise, face the void that creative blocks often leave. Stare into its depths and find the resolve to fill it with the creations only you can manifest.

- Use this time to question, challenge, and ultimately, to understand the nature of your creative impasse.

Cultivate Patience

- Recognize that creativity cannot be rushed. Allow yourself the grace of patience as you wait for the spark of inspiration to reignite.

- Understand that each moment of stillness brings you closer to the breakthrough you seek.

Engage in Creative Rituals

- Develop rituals that signal to your brain it's time to transition into a creative state. These rituals could be as simple as lighting a candle, brewing a cup of tea, or arranging your workspace.

- Rituals act as a bridge between the mundane and the magical, guiding you gently into the realm of creation.

Harness the Power of Reflection

- Use solitude as a mirror, reflecting on past successes and learning from previous obstacles.

- Analyze your creative process, identifying patterns that lead to blockages and strategizing ways to navigate around them in the future.

The Metamorphosis of Ideas

In the chrysalis of aloneness, ideas undergo a metamorphosis. What once was formless takes shape; what was once vague gains clarity. It is a process of becoming, of evolving beyond the confines of creative blocks into a realm of endless potential.

The Rebirth of Creativity

As you emerge from the cocoon of aloneness, you bring with you a rebirth of creativity. The blocks that once seemed insurmountable are now stepping stones to greater heights. With each step, you ascend to a new vantage point, where the horizon of your creative landscape expands, and the possibilities become as vast as the sky itself.

Chapter 14: The Spiritual Dimension of Aloneness

14.1 Aloneness in Spiritual Traditions

Aloneness has been held in high esteem throughout the ages and across diverse spiritual traditions. It is not a state of isolation but a sacred threshold where the divine communicates with the human soul, guiding it on its spiritual journey.

In the serene stillness of a Buddhist monastery, a monk sits in solitary meditation, the world around him a blur of impermanence. In the quiet recesses of a Christian mystic's cell, the boundaries between the self and the Savior dissolve in contemplative prayer. On a Sufi's solitary walk, each step is a dance with the Beloved, a silent rhythm that speaks of love beyond words.

These traditions, each in their way, honor aloneness as a spiritual practice, a pilgrimage to the inner sanctum. **Aloneness is a journey that requires no physical travel, for the destination is the heart, and the path is woven with the threads of solitude.**

Again:

Aloneness is a journey that requires no physical travel, for the destination is the heart, and the path is woven with the threads of solitude.

Buddhism teaches the art of detachment, where aloneness becomes a tool for understanding the transient nature of existence. Christian Mysticism finds in solitude the echo of God's voice, a call to union with the divine. Sufism celebrates aloneness as a lover's affair, where the soul meets the source of all love in the stillness of the heart.

In these sacred spaces of solitude, the spiritual seeker encounters the essence of being. **Aloneness is not a void but a vessel brimming with the nectar of spiritual insight, a chalice from which one sips the wine of enlightenment.**

14.2 Osho's Teachings on Spiritual Aloneness

Osho's teachings emerge as a profound exploration of aloneness in the vast expanse of spiritual discourse. His insights delve into the essence of spiritual solitude, where one discovers the boundless nature of existence.

Osho speaks of aloneness as the ultimate reality, where the individual transcends the ego and encounters the divine. **In his vision, aloneness is not a mere absence of others but a presence full of everything.** It is the ground on which the play of life unfolds, the space where the petals of the human spirit open to reveal the lotus of enlightenment.

Again:

Aloneness is not a mere absence of others but a presence full of everything.

Through his dynamic and often unconventional methods, Osho invites seekers to dance in the fire of aloneness, to let go of societal conditionings, and to embrace the freedom that comes with true solitude. **His teachings are not just doctrines but experiences, a series of experiments with one's consciousness.**

Osho's followers find a path to their innermost selves in spiritual aloneness. It is a journey that takes them through the layers of the mind, beyond the chatter and chaos, to a place of silence and serenity. **Here, in the sanctuary of solitude, the seeker is both the scientist and the subject, exploring the inner universe with the tools of awareness and presence.**

Osho's aloneness is a celebration, a festival of the self where every moment

is an opportunity to connect with the cosmic dance. **It is a call to awaken from the dream of separateness and realize that in aloneness, one is never alone.**
Again:

It is a call to awaken from the dream of separateness and realize that in aloneness, one is never alone.

14.3 Meditation and Contemplation

Meditation and contemplation arise as twin pillars supporting the seeker's journey toward inner truth in the sacred stillness of aloneness. These practices are the heartbeats of spiritual solitude. Each throbs a step deeper into the self and pauses for a moment of profound connection with the cosmos.

Meditation is the art of inner listening, a silent symphony where the soul's music is heard in its purest form. **It is a practice that transcends thought, where the mind's constant chatter gives way to the whisper of existence.** In the embrace of meditation, the seeker finds a still point, a center where the dance of life revolves in harmonious orbits.

Contemplation, its reflective counterpart, is the gaze turned inward, a contemplative embrace of life's mysteries. It is an introspective journey, where questions are more valuable than answers, and the seeking itself becomes the sacred destination.

Techniques:

- Meditation techniques vary from Vipassana's focused attention to the dynamic movement of Kundalini awakening. Each method offers a unique pathway to the same summit—the peak of self-awareness.
- Daily Practice involves integrating these techniques into the rhythm of everyday life, transforming routine into ritual and time into timeless.

In the solitude of meditation and contemplation, the seeker discovers the threads that weave the individual into the universal tapestry. **Aloneness becomes a crucible for transformation, a chalice brimming with the elixir**

of spiritual insight.

14.4 The Inner Journey

The inner journey is the quintessential pilgrimage of aloneness, a transformative voyage not across lands but through the layers of the self. It is a quest for the core, a descent into the heart of being where the true self resides in silent majesty.

This journey is solitary, for each traveler must navigate their path through the inner wilderness. The terrain is rich with the flora and fauna of emotions, thoughts, and memories. Here, in the depths of solitude, the seeker encounters the guardians of the psyche, each offering a riddle, a lesson, a key to deeper understanding.

The inner journey is marked by landmarks of transformation—moments of revelation, valleys of shadow, and peaks of clarity. It is a path that spirals inward, leading to the sacred center where the ego dissolves, and the spirit emerges in its purest form.

In this sacred aloneness, the seeker is both the map and the territory, the pilgrim and the shrine. With each step inward, the outer world's noise fades, and the voice of the inner guide grows more robust, more insistent. It is a voice that speaks not in words but in the language of intuition, a knowing that resonates with the vibration of truth.

The Inner Guide:

The inner guide is the seeker's constant companion, a presence that offers wisdom and comfort on the solitary road. The spark of divinity within, the inner guru, leads the way when the path becomes unclear, ensuring the seeker is never truly alone.

The Destination:

The destination of the inner journey is not a place but a state of being. It is the realization of oneness with all, the awakening to the interconnectedness of life. Here, in the aloneness of the inner sanctum, the seeker finds not isolation but a profound union with the cosmos.

14.5 The Universal Connection

The journey of aloneness culminates in the profound realization of the universal connection, a tapestry where every thread is an individual soul, and the entire weave is the cosmos itself.

In the sanctuary of solitude, the seeker understands that aloneness is the crucible in which the illusion of separation is melted away, revealing the pure gold of interconnectedness. It is a discovery that each solitary heartbeat echoes the rhythm of the universe, that every breath is a breeze in the vast expanse of existence.

Again:

In the sanctuary of solitude, the seeker understands that aloneness is the crucible in which the illusion of separation is melted away, revealing the pure gold of interconnectedness.

This universal connection is not an abstract concept but a living experience. It is felt in the quiet moments when the mind stills and the boundaries of the self blur and blend with the world around. **In this state, the seeker deeply empathizes with all living beings, a kinship that transcends language, culture, and creed.**

The Experience:

- The experience of this connection is both humbling and exalting. It humbles the seeker by showing them their place in the grand design, a single note in the symphony of creation. Yet, it exalts by revealing the intrinsic value of that note, the unique contribution of their presence to the harmony of the whole.

The Practice:

- The practice of recognizing the universal connection in aloneness becomes a daily ritual. It is found in the smile shared with a stranger, the compassion extended to another, and the silent acknowledgment of the sacredness of life.

In embracing the universal connection, the seeker's aloneness is transformed from a solitary journey into a shared voyage. They find that in reaching inward to the core of their being, they have reached outward to touch the essence of all beings. The realization dawns that in the heart of aloneness lies the seed of unity, and from this seed grows the tree of wisdom, its branches stretching into infinity, its roots anchored in the eternal truth of oneness.

Chapter 15: Overcoming Challenges on the Path to Aloneness

15.1 The Path's Intricacies

The journey towards embracing aloneness is a fascinating adventure, much like navigating a labyrinth. It is filled with twists and turns, each presenting its own set of challenges. The path to embracing aloneness is woven with intricacies, each twist and turn an invitation to deeper self-awareness and understanding. It is a journey that is as complex as it is rewarding, offering a tapestry of experiences that shape the seeker's soul.

The intricacies of the path are like the delicate threads of a spider's web, each one connected to the other, forming a pattern of stunning complexity and beauty. The seeker must navigate this web with care, for each decision, and each moment of reflection contributes to the integrity of the whole.

In the labyrinth of aloneness, the seeker encounters shadows and light, moments of doubt and revelations of truth. **It is a path that demands courage, for it requires one to face the self in its entirety—the light and the dark, the known and the unknown.**

The journey is self-reflective, a process of peering into the inner mirror and seeing the self in its rawest form. It is an odyssey that asks the seeker to be both the traveler and the mapmaker, empowering them to chart a course through the terrain of their own psyche.

Along the way, there are guideposts—moments of clarity where the path becomes clear, where the next step is illuminated by the light of inner wisdom. These guideposts could be a sudden realization about a personal pattern or a moment of profound understanding during a period of solitude. They are the seeker's allies, beacons that guide them through the fog of uncertainty. In embracing the intricacies of the path, the seeker learns to appreciate the journey's complexity. They understand that each intricacy is a lesson, a challenge, and an opportunity to grow. The path to aloneness is not a straight line but a spiral, leading ever inward to the heart of the self.

15.2 Identifying Challenges

Social Pressure:

The pressure to remain socially engaged can be overwhelming in a world that incessantly buzzes with connectivity. In the previous chapters, we have explored strategies to honor your inner call to aloneness, even when the world pulls you towards constant interaction.

Internal Resistance:

The quest for aloneness often meets with inner turmoil, a resistance born of ingrained beliefs and fears.

The path to embracing aloneness is strewn with challenges, each an obstacle that tests the seeker's resolve and commitment to the journey. **These challenges are not roadblocks but stepping stones, each offering a chance to rise and grow stronger.**

In the quietude of aloneness, the seeker may confront the challenge of social pressure, the weight of collective expectations pressing down like a heavy fog. **It is a test of will, a battle to maintain one's course when the world seems intent on steering you elsewhere.**

Then, there is the challenge of **internal resistance**, the inner voice of doubt that whispers loneliness and fear. **This voice is a siren call, luring the seeker back to the familiar shores of companionship and away from the solitary** depths where true self-discovery lies.

The Struggle:

The struggle with these challenges is not a sign of weakness but a necessary part of growth. It's a dance with one's shadows, a confrontation with the parts of the self that resist change and growth. It is a process of negotiation and understanding, a dialogue between the desire for solitude and the fear of isolation.

The Victory:

Victory over these challenges is not a conquest but a personal achievement, a harmonious balance between the need for aloneness and the reality of living in a connected world. **It is the art of standing firm in one's solitude while remaining open to the beauty of shared experience.** In identifying and facing these challenges, the seeker learns the true meaning of strength. It is not the absence of fear but the presence of courage, the ability to move forward even when the path is uncertain. **This commitment to facing challenges will lead to personal growth and self-discovery.**

15.3 Strategies for Overcoming Challenges

Mindfulness:

Cultivate the art of Mindfulness, a practice that illuminates the present moment, revealing the times when we subconsciously shun solitude. Through Mindfulness, we learn to recognize and transform our patterns of avoidance into acceptance.

Small Steps:

Embrace solitude in increments, allowing yourself to acclimate to the stillness of being alone. This gradual approach fosters a sense of security within solitude, slowly building a sanctuary of peace in your presence.

Support System:

Surround yourself with a circle of understanding—a support system that not only respects your need for solitude but also encourages it. **Their support becomes a bastion of strength when the tides of challenges rise, making you feel valued and understood.**

Challenges mark the seeker's journey through aloneness, but with each obstacle comes a strategy for transcendence, a method to turn trials into triumphs.

As mentioned in previous chapters, when faced with the challenge of social pressure, the seeker can employ the strategy of **Mindfulness**. This practice anchors them in the present moment, allowing them to observe societal expectations without being swayed by them. Mindfulness becomes a shield, deflecting the external noise and fostering a serene inner clarity.

Meditation is the strategy to counter internal resistance. Through meditation, the seeker engages in a dialogue with their inner self, soothing the fears and calming the doubts that arise from solitude. It is a process of gentle persuasion, where the resistant parts of the self are met with compassion and understanding.

To recapitulate...

The Tools:

- **Mindfulness** practices include breathing exercises and mindful observation, which ground the seeker in the reality of the now, providing a bulwark against the onslaught of social demands.

- **Meditation** offers a variety of approaches, from guided visualizations to silent sitting, each a pathway to inner peace and resolve.

The Application:

- These strategies are not one-time applications but daily practices woven into the fabric of the seeker's life. They become habits, second nature, a part of the seeker's very being.

In employing these strategies, the seeker transforms the path of aloneness from a solitary trek into a journey of empowerment. Each challenge overcome is a victory, a testament to the seeker's strength and dedication to the pursuit of aloneness as a spiritual practice.

15.4 Learning from Setbacks

The path of aloneness is not without its setbacks, but within each apparent defeat lies a lesson waiting to be learned, a hidden gem of wisdom to be uncovered.

Setbacks on this journey are not failures but signposts, each pointing toward a deeper understanding of the self and the nature of solitude. They are the unexpected teachers, the harsh tutors that test the seeker's resolve and resilience.

Reflect on Experiences:

View setbacks not as failures but as stepping stones for growth. Reflect on each experience's lessons, and recalibrate your journey towards aloneness with newfound insights.

When setbacks occur, the seeker is invited to reflect on their experiences, look back compassionately, and understand what led to the stumble. This reflection is not an exercise in self-reproach but a gentle inquiry into the self, a learning process that fosters growth and self-compassion.

Resilience:

Fortify your resolve with resilience, reminding yourself of the tranquility and self-discovery that aloneness brings. Each step forward, no matter how small, is progress toward inner peace. Resilience is the fruit of these reflections, a strength forged in the fires of adversity. It is the ability to rise after a fall, dust oneself off, and continue with renewed determination and insight.

The Process:

- Learning from setbacks involves acknowledging the pain, embracing the discomfort, and finding the courage to move forward. **It is a dance with one's vulnerabilities, a choreography of recovery and grace.**

In learning from setbacks, the seeker discovers the true meaning of progress. It is not measured by the absence of obstacles but by the ability to overcome them. Each setback becomes a stepping stone, each lesson a milestone on the road to mastering the art of aloneness.

15.5 Maintaining the Practice

Routine:

Anchor your practice of aloneness in routine, creating a rhythmic flow that integrates aloneness into the fabric of daily life. This routine becomes the heartbeat of your journey, steady and reassuring.

Establishing a routine is crucial. It provides structure, a framework within which the practice of aloneness can flourish. This routine might involve setting aside a specific time each day for meditation, journaling, or simply being in silence.

Flexibility:

Embrace flexibility, allowing your practice to ebb and flow with the currents of life. Adaptability ensures that the essence of aloneness remains intact, even as the external circumstances shift.

However, rigidity can stifle growth, so flexibility is equally important. The seeker must be willing to adjust their practice as life's circumstances change, embracing the ebb and flow of existence without losing sight of their commitment to solitude.

Balance:

The balance between routine and flexibility is the dance of maintenance. It is an understanding that while habits are powerful, the ability to adapt allows the practice to thrive in the long term.

The practice of aloneness, like any profound discipline, requires consistency and adaptability. It is a commitment that must be nurtured and maintained to yield the rich fruits of solitude.

Maintaining the practice of aloneness is akin to tending a garden. It requires regular attention, care, and the willingness to adapt to the changing seasons of life. The seeker must cultivate their solitude with intention, watering it with moments of quiet reflection and fertilizing it with the richness of their experiences.

In maintaining the practice of aloneness, the seeker finds a steady rhythm, a heartbeat that pulses with the quiet joy of solitude. It is a practice that becomes a part of who they are, a sanctuary within themselves, no matter where they go or what they do.

Conclusion

To walk the path of aloneness is to embark on an odyssey of the soul, a pilgrimage to the core of one's being. It is a path strewn with challenges yet rich with the rewards of self-discovery and inner harmony. **As we draw the curtains on this exploration of aloneness, let us remember that the journey of aloneness is a canvas upon which we paint the story of our lives.** Each moment of aloneness is a stroke of the brush, each silent reflection a hue that adds depth and texture to the masterpiece that is our existence. **Your journey of self-discovery is not just unique; it is invaluable and irreplaceable.**

Let this book be a compass that guides you through the ebbs and flows of aloneness, a testament to the enduring spirit of those who seek solace in their own company. May this book serve as a beacon of encouragement, a reminder that the journey of aloneness, though solitary, is one of the most profound adventures of the human experience. **Herein lies the wisdom to transform aloneness from a state of unwanted and dreary predicament to a state of blissful becoming, a journey not just to be alone but to be whole.** Embrace this path, for it is a journey of transformation worthy of the pages of a bestseller and, even more so, of the chapters of your life.

You, the seeker, are the author of this grand narrative. Your life is the book and aloneness—the sacred ink with which you inscribe your tale. It is a story of discovery, battles fought and won in the quiet corners of your soul: hope, love and desire, joy, creativity, authenticity, and fun, all written in the indelible ink of aloneness.

Let aloneness be your muse, guide, and companion on this odyssey. **Embrace it with open arms, for it is in the quiet moments alone that the whispers of your heart are heard most clearly.** In the embrace of aloneness, it is here that you find the freedom to be authentically you, unbound by the expectations of others, true to the rhythm of your spirit, and aligned with the Source within. **Remember that you are COMPLETE. Remember that you are WORTHY, and your worthiness should not be questioned or doubted.**

Again:

Remember that you are COMPLETE. Remember that you are WORTHY, and your worthiness should not be questioned or doubted.

So go forth, bold traveler, with the quill of aloneness in hand. Write your story with courage, with honesty, with love. In this tapestry that you weave, you see not just a story of solitude but a **masterpiece of connection**—a symphony of experiences that sings of the connectedness of you with everything else. **For it is in going deep into your aloneness that you will realize that you are connected with everything else.**

Again, for the last time:

For it is in going deep into your aloneness that you will realize that you are connected with everything else.

REMEMBER:

You are the author of your story; let aloneness be the ink with which you write a MASTERPIECE.

Good job. Now the journey begins...

Be A Co-Creator With Me

B E A CO-CREATOR WITH ME

Now, you are more equipped to find love, creativity, and authenticity within. It's time to pass on your newfound knowledge and wisdom and show other readers where they can see the same help.

Please do a Review of this book from the Store or Online Store where you bought this book. Doing a Review is more than just a generous gesture. It's a valuable initiative that can guide other readers, from Baby Boomers to Gen Zers, to find the information they're looking for and discover the true value of Aloneness.

Thank you for your invaluable help and for being a Co-Creator with me. Your doing a Review keeps the spirit of this book, "Osho's Wisdom on Aloneness," alive and is a vital part of passing on our collective knowledge and wisdom.

I deeply appreciate your kind gesture.

References

- *Osho on Aloneness* https://www.osho.com/read/osho/osho-on-topics/alonen ess
- *Aloneness – Loneliness – Solitude? – OSHO Online Library* https://www.osho. com/osho-online-library/osho-talks/aloneness-loneliness-solitude-a8 ad9789-70a?p=608d0332a9ff492f2a5ea7a67a5dcc6e
- *Knowing Your Aloneness* https://oshoworld.com/knowing-your-aloneness/
- *Aloneness – Loneliness – Relating? – OSHO Online Library* https://www.osh o.com/osho-online-library/osho-talks/aloneness-loneliness-relating-e f0b8133-abd?p=f4ed979781e180913205e983197243bb
- *Generations – Research and Data from Pew Research Center* https://www.pe wreaserchcenter.org/topic/generations-age/generations/
- *From Loneliness to Aloneness | Osho News* https://oshonews.com/2017/09/ 22/from-loneliness-to-aloneness
- *Find Yourself in Aloneness | Osho News* https://oshonews.com/2019/07/22/ find-yourself-in-aloneness
- *Become Strong and Confident from Within – OSHOTimes* https://www.oshoti mes.com/insights/lifestyle/love/become-strong-and-confident-from- within
- *Acceptance – Anxiety – Unconditional? – OSHO Online Library* https://www. osho.com/osho-online-library/osho-talks/
- *Freedom, Aloneness, Rebellion* https://www.osho.com/osho-online-librar y/osho-talks/freedom-aloneness-rebellion-271618b3-722?p=e20b25bb

6a11acc1a976e91c6eeef1a4

- *Love, Freedom, Aloneness: The Koan of Relationships* https://bookclubs.com/books/love-freedom-aloneness-the-koan-of-relationships-18727
- *Loneliness is Pain, Aloneness is Peace* https://www.osho.com/read/featured-articles/other-myself/loneliness-is-pain-alone-ness-is-peace-hmm
- *Being Alone, Being Lonely: Osho Explains the Difference* https://completewellbeing.com/article/being-alone-being-lonely-osho-explains-difference/
- *Aloneness, Nothingness, Loneliness* https://www.osho.com/osho-online-library/osho-talks/aloneness-nothingness-loneliness-45bf795e-042?p=4232b09ebbc6af8520fcefb0a7498b5b
- *Embracing Wisdom: The Four Agreements* https://www.avlf.com/books/embracing-wisdom-the-four-agreements/
- *Eastern Philosophy vs Western Philosophy: Exploring Cultural Perspectives on Life and Knowledge* https://overtimephilosophy.com/eastern-philosophy-vs-western-philosophy-exploring-cultural-perspectives-on-life-and-knowledge/
- *Everything You Need to Know About Osho Philosophy and the Teachings* https://yourviews.mindstick.com/view/85362/everything-you-need-to-know-about-osho-philosophy-and-the-teachings
- *The Dance of Aloneness, The Song of Awareness* https://oshoworld.com/the-dance-of-aloneness-the-song-of-awareness/
- *Osho: 10 Key Teachings from the Indian Philosopher and Poet* https://www.discoverwalks.com/blog/india/osho-10-key-teachings-from-the-indian-philosopher-and-poet/
- *Osho: Being Alone* https://completewellbeing.com/article/osho-being-alone/
- *Quotes About Darkness Within* https://www.moneyjojo.com/quotes/quotes-about-darkness-within/
- *Osho Yoga* https://archive.org/details/oshoYoga
- *Bhagwan Shree Rajneesh* https://simple.wikipedia.org/wiki/Bhagwan_Shree_Rajneesh
- *Chhandogya Upanishad* https://www.swami-krishnananda.org/chhand/C

hhandogya_Upanishad.pdf

- *Art of Meditation, Freedom, Aloneness* https://www.osho.com/osho-online-library/osho-talks/art-of-meditation-freedom-aloneness-fdb8a887-f0a?p=d24d82c633d582058e58be249a5be00a
- *Love, Freedom, Aloneness* https://archive.org/details/lovefreedomalone00osho
- *Agile Alchemy* https://industry40.com/2023/12/08/agile-alchemy/
- *Osho: Meditating on the Night* https://www.oshoteachings.com/osho-meditating-on-the-night/
- *All About Osho* https://www.osho.com/allaboutosho/
- *Exploring the Spiritual Practices of Osho Rajneesh: A Journey into Dynamic Meditation and Sannyas* https://cultureandheritage.org/2024/03/exploring-the-spiritual-practices-of-osho-rajneesh-a-journey-into-dynamic-meditation-and-sannyas.html
- *The Self, Inner Being, Solitude* https://www.osho.com/osho-online-library/osho-talks/the-self-inner-being-solitude-04699316-3a3?p=a7b75f556899c6503698d8caa1ec47ad
- *Osho Quotes and Teachings* https://www.dailymoss.com/osho-quotes-teachings/
- *Osho on Creativity* https://www.osho.com/read/osho/osho-on-topics/creativity
- *Creativity: Doing Things Joyfully and Lovingly* https://oshoworld.com/creativity-doing-things-joyfully-and-lovingly/
- *What Does Wellness Really Mean* https://www.osho.com/newsletters/what-does-wellness-really-mean
- *Osho on Healing* https://www.osho.com/read/osho/osho-on-topics/healing
- *Life's Mysteries: Intro Osho* https://www.oshonews.com/2014/05/27/lifes-mysteries-intro-osho/
- *Aloneness, Loneliness, Solitude* https://www.osho.com/osho-online-library/osho-talks/aloneness-loneliness-solitude-a8ad9789-70a?p=608d0332a9ff492f2a5ea7a67a5dcc6e
- *Seeking Sake Flavour Profiles* https://spectrum.global/blog/event/seeking-

sake-flavour-profiles/

About the Author

Born and raised in the Philippines, Alden Clamor graduated with an AB in Psychology from the Ateneo de Manila University. After graduation, he moved to Europe, where he spent the next 10 years dividing his time between Paris, France, and Brussels, Belgium. While in Paris, he studied French, which is why he now speaks French like a local French guy. When he returned to the Philippines, he pursued nursing, successfully graduated with a BS in Nursing from UDMC (now SACI), and passed the Nursing Board Exam. He ranked in the Top 11 of his nursing batch. However, rather than working in a hospital to be an appendage of a doctor, he chose to use his healthcare knowledge to prioritize and reinforce his health and the health of others willing to listen. Through his work as an author, publisher, and digital storyteller, he now impacts a broader range of people with his message of health, hope, sovereignty, and restoration.

Also by Alden Clamor

The books below are EXCELLENT companions for this book and will supplement and deepen your understanding of self-compassion and self-love. I highly recommend that you add them to your precious collection.

Don't Be Afraid of Loving Yourself: The Art of Loving Yourself According To Osho

In a world brimming with self-doubt and societal pressures, this book emerges as a beacon of hope. This transformative guide is a journey toward self-compassion, authenticity, and inner peace. Crafted for the ambitious Millennials, the curious Gen Z, and the introspective Gen X, this book is a call to action for anyone who has ever felt hindered by their own self-judgment. With actionable steps, you'll learn to navigate life's challenges with equanimity, grace and self-love.

Nobody Told You EVER About This Before

This book is a unique blend of brain health nurturing, mental resilience enhancement, shadow work journaling, the law of attraction and the power of belief as taught by Abraham-Hicks. The 5 Ninja hacks or life hacks enumerated in this book will empower you with confidence, peace of mind, mental wellness, robust health and self esteem. Structured to walk you through each aspect of your wellness journey, the book is divided into comprehensive chapters that cover these important life hacks. Each section includes exercises, reflective questions, and actionable steps designed to be easily integrated into your daily life, encouraging you to engage and apply what you learn actively.

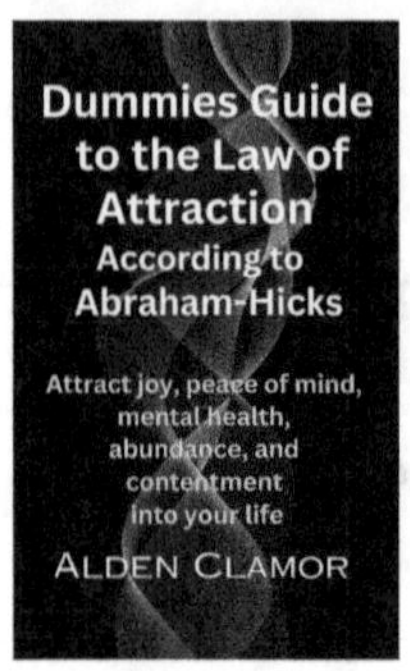

Dummies Guide to the Law of Attraction According to Abraham-Hick: Attract joy, peace of mind, abundance, and contentment into your life

For those who belong to that ever-expanding circle of friends, this next sentence will explain why I wrote this book: "I am a raving fan of Abraham-Hicks". A few years ago, I decided to go to the Abraham-Hicks Website and purchase the Getting Into the Vortex Meditation Guide. I started to meditate. My life just started to metamorphose. It's like coming from a dark cave into the sunlight.

"Coming from the cave and stepping into the sunlight", that's how I would describe my awakening. This book is a sharing of the stuff that I have learned. This book is a sharing of the principles I have learned to apply. This book is a sharing of the "No-Nos" I have learned to watch out for in order to live a satisfying life. Frankly, this book is really a guide for me so I will not forget the stuff that I have learned. But since we are all in this together, I reckon I can share the stuff with you too.

Osho's Wisdom on Aloneness (FRENCH VERSION)

Libérez la sagesse profonde des enseignements d'Osho et découvrez le pouvoir éclairant de la solitude. Trouvez la sérénité dans la solitude, même si vous l'avez toujours associée à la solitude.

"La sagesse d'Osho sur la solitude : l'art d'être seul selon Osho" propose une exploration de la solitude loin de la stigmatisation sociétale de la solitude. Vous bénéficierez d'un compagnon dévoué qui vous fournira des idées réconfortantes et des stratégies transformatrices pour faire de la solitude une source de paix durable, d'auto-compassion, de créativité, d'authenticité et d'immense croissance personnelle.

Osho's Wisdom on Aloneness (SPANISH VERSION)

Descubra la profunda sabiduría de las enseñanzas de Osho y el poder iluminador de la soledad. Encuentre la serenidad en la soledad, incluso si siempre la ha asociado con la soledad.

¿A menudo anhela la soledad, pero siente que está en conflicto con las expectativas sociales de sociabilidad?

"La sabiduría de Osho sobre la soledad: el arte de estar solo según Osho" ofrece una exploración de la soledad lejos del estigma social de la soledad. Tendrás un compañero dedicado que te brindará perspectivas reconfortantes y estrategias transformadoras para hacer de la soledad una fuente de paz duradera, autocompasión, creatividad, autenticidad y un inmenso crecimiento personal.